A Crash Course
in Statistics

Sara Miller McCune founded SAGE Publishing in 1965 to support the dissemination of usable knowledge and educate a global community. SAGE publishes more than 1000 journals and over 800 new books each year, spanning a wide range of subject areas. Our growing selection of library products includes archives, data, case studies and video. SAGE remains majority owned by our founder and after her lifetime will become owned by a charitable trust that secures the company's continued independence.

Los Angeles | London | New Delhi | Singapore | Washington DC | Melbourne

A Crash Course in Statistics

Ryan J. Winter

Florida International University

Los Angeles | London | New Delhi
Singapore | Washington DC | Melbourne

FOR INFORMATION:

SAGE Publications, Inc.
2455 Teller Road
Thousand Oaks, California 91320
E-mail: order@sagepub.com

SAGE Publications Ltd.
1 Oliver's Yard
55 City Road
London EC1Y 1SP
United Kingdom

SAGE Publications India Pvt. Ltd.
B 1/I 1 Mohan Cooperative Industrial Area
Mathura Road, New Delhi 110 044
India

SAGE Publications Asia-Pacific Pte. Ltd.
3 Church Street
#10–04 Samsung Hub
Singapore 049483

ISBN 978-1-5443-0704-6

Acquisitions Editor: Helen Salmon
Editorial Assistant: Chelsea Neve
Production Editor: Nevair Kabakian
Copy Editor: Sarah J. Duffy
Typesetter: C&M Digitals (P) Ltd.
Proofreader: Caryne Brown
Cover Designer: India (Design), SAGE
Marketing Manager: Shari Countryman

17 18 19 20 21 10 9 8 7 6 5 4 3 2 1

TABLE OF CONTENTS

An SPSS data file to run the examples included in this book can be downloaded from the book's website at **study/sagepub.com/winter**

ABOUT THE AUTHOR

Dr. Ryan J. Winter conducts research on the relationship between psychology and legal issues, focusing in part on jury decision making. He has investigated jurors' comprehension of death penalty instructions, jurors' use of inadmissible evidence, bilingualism in jurors, and how jurors make liability and damage award determinations in civil cases. Dr. Winter's research also focuses on legal decisions in sexual harassment cases. Courses he has taught include Social Psychology, Trial Consulting, Psychology and Law, and Social Cognition. He received his PhD from the City University of New York and his Master's of Legal Studies degree from the University of Nebraska–Lincoln. He is currently the research methods coordinator for the Florida International University Psychology Department.

DESCRIPTIVE STATISTICS

What follows is a quick reminder of descriptive statistics. Quiz yourself on descriptive statistics at the end of this chapter! You can run all the examples in this book using a data file posted at the website: **study.sagepub.com/winter**

HOW, WHEN, AND WHY DO WE USE DESCRIPTIVE STATISTICS?

First, let's make sure you understand the concept of *descriptive statistics*. As you can probably figure out based on the name, descriptive statistics describe the data. There are three essential characteristics of descriptive statistics we need to discuss: scales of measurement, measures of central tendency, and measures of variability (or spread).

1. Scales of measurement are different ways to classify the measurement of a study variable. There are four categories we will consider: nominal scales, ordinal scales, interval scales, and ratio scales.

    Nominal scales are based on assigning items to categories. For example, you can have yes versus no categories, or male versus female categories, or Honda versus Toyota versus Subaru versus Ford. For nominal scales, there is no better or worse, higher or lower—just different categories. (After all, which is higher: males or females?)

    Ordinal scales have more order to them. That is, they are ranked. Thus there might be a better or worse ranking here (pizza is ranked highest, salad second highest, sandwiches third highest, haggis lowest for food preference). We might know the order, but we may not know how spread out those preferences are. That is, maybe pizza, salad, and sandwiches are all ranked very high in preference but haggis is ranked really, really low! Or think about a marathon race. The first, second, and third place finishers may come in a few seconds apart while the fourth place finisher is more than a minute behind.

Interval scales have order and equal intervals between items. That is, we can look at a scale ("Rank this food on a scale from 1 to 9, with 1 being not at all preferred and 9 being highly preferred"). Here, we have order: 9 is high while 1 is low. We also know that the difference between 1 and 2 is the same as the difference between 8 and 9. There are set distances between all numbers that are always equal.

Ratio scales have order, equal intervals, and a zero point. A zero indicates a total lack of the property. For example, you can get 0 correct on a 10-question test. Correctness can thus range from 0 to 10, but it cannot go below 0. It still has order (5 correct is higher than 3 correct) and intervals (the difference between 1 and 3 correct is the same as the difference between 6 and 8 correct). Time is another good ratio—there can be a zero time, but you cannot go below "no time."

2. Measures of central tendency refer to a single score that shows the central number in a set of numbers. I bet you already know these! There are three kinds of central tendency measurements: mode, median, and mean.

The **mode** refers to the most frequently occurring number. In the set of numbers 12, 15, 15, 17, 18, 20, the mode is 15. In some cases, we may have multiple modes. For the set of numbers 12, 15, 15, 17, 17, 18, 20, we have a bimodal set (both 15 and 17 are modes). We use modes mostly for nominal scales (if participants are male, male, male, female, female, male, then our mode is male—this gender occurs 4 out of 6 times).

The **median** refers to the middle number. In the set 12, 15, 15, 17, 17, 18, 20, our median is 17 (12, 15, and 15 come before it, while 17, 18, and 20 come after it). In the set 12, 15, 15, 17, 18, 20, there are two central numbers: 15 and 17. We simply 15 + 17, and then divide by 2. 15 + 17 = 32 / 2 = 16. We can use the median for ordinal, interval, and ratio scales (since all are based on order).

The **mean** is the average number. In the set 12, 15, 15, 17, 17, 18, 20, the mean is 16.29. That is, 12 + 15 + 15 + 17 + 17 + 18 + 20 = 114 / 7 =

16.29. We use the mean only for interval and ratio data since we need scale items to have equal intervals.

3. Measures of variability (or measure of spread) tell us how numbers spread out around the mean. That is, how much do they vary? There are three kinds of variability I want to discuss here: range, variance, and standard deviation.

   The **range** is the simplest measure of variability. You simply subtract the lowest score from the highest score. In the set 12, 15, 15, 17, 17, 18, 20, the range is 20 minus 12, or 8. Unfortunately, it doesn't tell us much more than the highest and lowest number, and thus it is susceptible to outlier issues. In the set 12, 15, 15, 17, 17, 18, 15,000, the range is 14,988, but that last number is huge! It is somewhat misleading to keep this large number in the data set as most numbers are within 12 to 18.

   Variance tells us about the variation in the data set. The larger the number, the more variability. Finding variance is the first step in looking at the standard deviation.

   The **standard deviation** is the square root of the variance. This is the statistic you will use frequently when discussing your descriptive statistics. It relates to the normal curve, which you can see in the following figure.

FIGURE 1.1

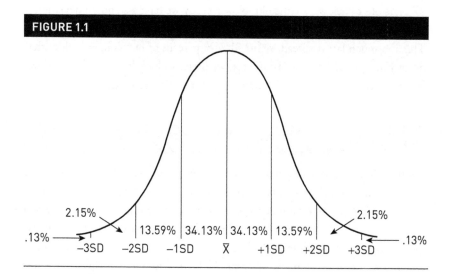

Let's say we have a normal curve that represents 100% of all cases in our sample. Fifty percent fall at or below the mean, while 50% are at or above the mean. The standard deviation (SD) breaks this down even further. That is, 34.13% of all cases fall between the mean and one standard deviation above the mean. In addition, 34.13% of all cases fall between the mean and one standard deviation below the mean. Thus 68.26% of all cases fall between minus one and plus one standard deviations of the mean. For two standard deviations, another 13.59% of the sample is counted. That is, if we look at two standard deviations above and below the mean, this accounts for 95.44% of the sample (13.59 + 34.13 + 34.13 + 13.59 = 95.44). Three SDs adds another 2.15 on each end, and so on.

What the standard deviation tells us is how many participants fall within that percentage. Think about age of participants. Imagine we have a sample ranging from 10 to 36 years old. It's a big range, right (36 − 10 = 26)? Further imagine that our mean (average) age is 24. If we know the standard deviation, we have even more information about the sample. Let's say our standard deviation is 3 years (which we get by calculating the variance from a set of participant ages and taking the square root). If one standard deviation is 3 years, and our mean age is 24, then we know that 34.13% of our sample ranges in age from 24 to 27 (the mean + the standard deviation, or 24 + 3 = 27). We also know that 34.13% of our sample ranges from 21 to 24 (the mean minus the standard deviation, or 24 − 3 = 21). Thus we know that 68.26% of our sample ranges in age from 21 to 27 (mean of 24 +/− 3). As you can see, a standard deviation of 3 shows that a lot of our sample clusters around that young adult range. Only 31.74% falls above 27 years old or below 21 years old. Now let's say we have a standard deviation of 10 with a mean of 24. Here, 68.26% of our sample ranges in age from 14 to 34. This is a much larger spread, right? 31.74% percent of our sample is older than 34 or younger than 14. As researchers, we prefer to have less spread, as it shows less variance overall, i.e. give us more precise statistical estimates.

An Example: Social Influence and College Textbooks

A robust finding in social psychology is that when people have insufficient information about how to behave or what decision to make, they rely on others as a source of information. Imagine we ask college student participants how much money they spent on books last semester. We have them fill out their name and the amount of money they recall spending at the bottom of a book survey after the names and amounts listed by 10 prior participants. Unknown to our participants, we alter the amounts recalled by the 10 prior participants, creating one condition with a high average book price ($150) and one condition with a low average book price ($75). We predict that those who see high dollar amounts from prior participants will use that information as an anchor point and recall spending a similar high amount themselves. Those in our low dollar amount condition will anchor to that lower amount. We collect signatures and dollar amounts from 10 real participants randomly assigned to the High Dollar (HD) condition and 10 real participants randomly assigned to the Low Dollar (LD) condition. Consider the data:

High Dollar Condition ($)	Low Dollar Condition ($)
134	77
156	65
134	87
132	100
164	88
127	68
135	86
134	73
133	69
151	87
$\Sigma HD = 1,400$	$\Sigma LD = 800$
Mean = 140	Mean = 80
Median = 134	Median = 81.5
Mode = 134	Mode = 87
Standard Deviation = 12.33	Standard Deviation = 11.28

Σ, or the symbol for Sigma, means "the sum of." Thus Σ_{HD} is the sum of the scores for the High Dollar Condition. That is, 134 + 156 + 134 + 132 + 164 + 127 + 135 + 134 + 133 + 151 = 1,400. There are 10 scores here, so we divide 1,400 by 10 to get 140, our mean. The median is the middle number (in this case 134 + 134 / 2 = 134). The mode is the most frequently occurring number (in this case 134 appears three times). The standard deviation is 12.33, which means that 34.13% of all scores fall between the mean (140) and 1 standard deviation above the mean (140 + 12.33 = 152.33), while another 34.13% falls between the mean (140) and 1 standard deviation below the mean (140 – 12.33 = 127.67). Thus 68.26% of the sample in the High Dollar Condition recalled spending between $128 and $152, which is close to our high dollar anchor amount of $150.

We do the same thing for the Low Dollar Condition, giving us a mean of 80 (800 / 10 = 80), a median of 81.5 (77 + 86 / 2 = 81.5), and a mode of 87. Our standard deviation is 11.28, with most Low Dollar Condition participants (68.26%) recalling spending between $68.72 and $91.28 on their books (once again, pretty close to our low anchor). Keep in mind that the variance here is the standard deviation squared, or 11.28 × 11.28 = 127.23. Since variance is not on the same scale as the standard deviation, it is less useful in psychology studies.

Let's run this in SPSS. There are several different ways to get descriptives, so we'll look at three different SPSS procedures: means, descriptives, and frequencies. **(Note: If you are writing a participant section, I highly recommend frequencies.)**

1. SPSS: OUR BOOK SURVEY STUDY (USING THE MEANS PROCEDURE)

1. The first method I want to show you has the advantage of looking at means and standard deviations within different levels of the independent variable. That is, maybe I want to see the mean and SD for the High Dollar Condition compared to the Low Dollar Condition. To run this test, you should use the Means procedure. First, click Analyze > Compare Means > Means . . . on the top menu as shown in the following screenshot.

You will be presented with the following:

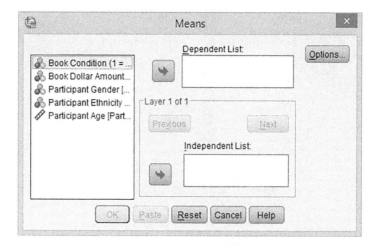

2. Put the **Book Condition (1 High, 2 Low)** variable into the Independent List box and the **Book Dollar Amount (in $)** variable into the Dependent List box by highlighting the relevant variables and pressing the ⬛ buttons.

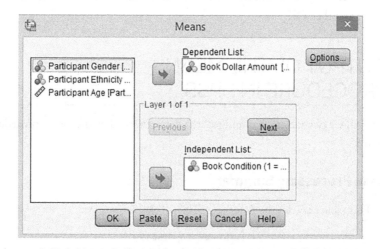

3. Next, click the Options button.

You will be presented with the following screen:

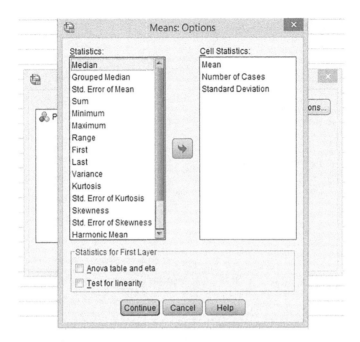

4. As you can see, the Mean, Number of Cases, and Standard Deviation are preselected for you. You can get other statistics if you want from the left column, but we will stick with those three items only. Select Continue and then OK.

OUTPUT OF THE MEANS PROCEDURE IN SPSS

You will see two tables containing all the data generated by the means procedure in SPSS.

Case Processing Summary

This table provides the *N* for us. It isn't all that important.

Case Processing Summary

	Cases					
	Included		Excluded		Total	
	N	Percent	N	Percent	N	Percent
Book Dollar Amount * Book Condition (1 = High, 2 - Low)	20	100.0%	0	0.0%	20	100.0%

Report

The report, however, gives us our mean and standard deviation for each group (high and low) as well as the total mean and standard deviation across condition. (Please note this Total row, as we will discuss it in our next few procedures).

Report

Book Dollar Amount

Book Condition (1 = High, 2 - Low)	Mean	N	Std. Deviation
High	140.00	10	12.329
Low	80.00	10	11.284
Total	110.00	20	32.859

REPORTING THE OUTPUT FOR THE MEANS PROCEDURE

We report the statistics in this format:

Students in the High Dollar Condition recalled spending an average of $140 (SD = 12.33) on books. Students in the Low Dollar Condition recalled spending an average of $80 (SD = 11.28).

That's our first way of getting means. Not too hard, right? When getting the mean and standard deviation for interval- or ratio-dependent variables like dollar amount, time, height, and weight, the Means procedure is useful. Of course, there are other ways of getting descriptive statistics that are a part of other statistical tests. For example, when running a t-test or an ANOVA, descriptives may be automatically given to you in the output, or you can click on the Options button in those SPSS menus to get means, standard deviations, and ranges.

However, let's say you don't want to look at dollar amounts recalled across different conditions. You can still use the Means procedure, but this time leave the Independent List box empty. You can then see the total mean and standard deviation across all participants (not separated by High or Low Dollar Condition). For example, the mean across all participants in the book survey study is $110 (SD = 32.86). An alternative way to look at descriptives is by using the Descriptives procedure in SPSS. It will similarly give you descriptive information for the entire sample (not broken up by condition)

2. SPSS: OUR BOOK STUDY (USING THE DESCRIPTIVES PROCEDURE)

1. Click Analyze > Descriptive Statistics > Descriptives . . . on the top menu as shown in the following screenshot.

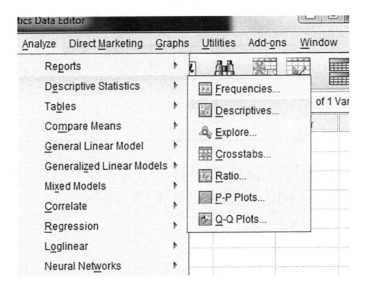

You will be presented with the following (notice there is no longer an Independent List box):

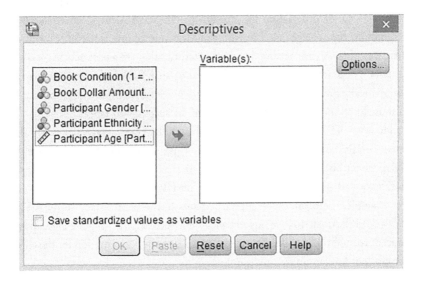

We will move variables that we want descriptive statistics for over to the Variable(s) box. In this case, we can look at several dependent variables (Book Dollar Amount, Participant Gender, Participant Ethnicity, and Participant age). Let's move all of our dependent variables over . . .

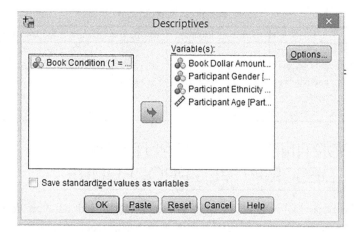

Now, click on Options. You will see several potential choices. Click the ones I chose.

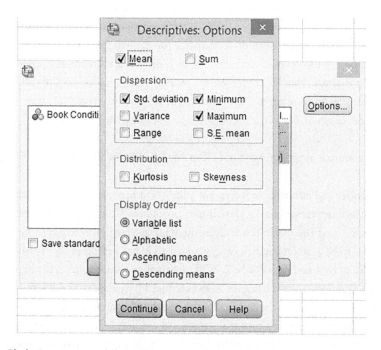

Click Continue, and then OK.

OUTPUT OF THE DESCRIPTIVES PROCEDURE IN SPSS

When using Descriptives, you will see only one box.

Descriptive Statistics

	N	Minimum	Maximum	Mean	Std. Deviation
Book Dollar Amount	20	65	164	110.00	32.859
Participant Gender	20	1.00	2.00	1.5500	.51042
Participant Ethnicity	20	1.00	4.00	2.0500	1.05006
Participant Age	20	18.00	24.00	20.3500	2.03328
Valid N (listwise)	20				

REPORTING THE OUTPUT FOR THE DESCRIPTIVES PROCEDURE

See the Book Dollar Amount row? The mean (110) and standard deviation (32.86) here are identical to the Total from the means report we saw in our prior test (the Means procedure). We don't get the information separately for the High and Low Dollar Conditions. This is a limitation of the Descriptives procedure in SPSS when you want to look within different levels of your independent variable.

But consider our next three rows related to participant gender, ethnicity, and age. We often report descriptive statistics for demographic information, but I hope you see the problem with looking at gender and ethnicity here. Before we look at that problem, let's first look at age. As you can see, our sample ranged in age from 18 (minimum) to 24 (maximum). The mean age was 20.35 with a standard deviation of 2.03. In a results section, I would write this as follows:

The sample ranged in age from 18 to 24 ($M = 20.35$, $SD = 2.03$).

Gender and ethnicity, however, are a little odd here and are actually inappropriate to interpret within the Descriptives procedure. Consider gender. The minimum is 1 and the maximum is 2. In my data set, I assigned males to be 1 and females to be 2, so obviously it ranges from 1 to 2, but I could easily have assigned females to be 1 and males to be 2. With nominal scales, we aren't really interested in the numbers, just the category. Also note that I have a mean of 1.55 for gender, but does that make any sense? Is there any such thing as an average gender? Not really, right? Gender is a nominal variable (a category). The same thing applies to ethnicity. Our average ethnicity here is 2.05, but since I have five categories (Caucasian, African American, Hispanic/Latino, Asian, and Other), an average ethnicity of 2.05 is meaningless. We cannot use the mean for gender or ethnicity. Instead, we rely on the mode, which tells us how many data points fall into each category—that is, how many men are there and how many women are there, and how many of each ethnicity are represented? To get the mode, we need to run a different type of SPSS test: Frequencies.

3. SPSS: OUR BOOK STUDY (USING THE FREQUENCIES PROCEDURE)

1. Click Analyze > Descriptive Statistics > Frequencies . . . on the top menu as shown in the following screenshot.

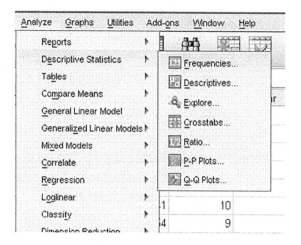

You will be presented with the following:

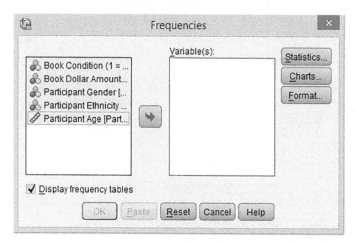

As with the Descriptives procedure, move the variables that we want descriptive statistics for over to the Variable(s) box. In this case, I prefer to look at my dependent variables (Book Dollar Amount, Participant Gender, Participant Ethnicity, Participant Age). Again, you should notice that there is no place to list your independent variable in this Frequencies procedure. Thus you will not be able to get means and standard deviations for each of your separate conditions (High versus Low). For now, move all of the dependent variables to the variables box.

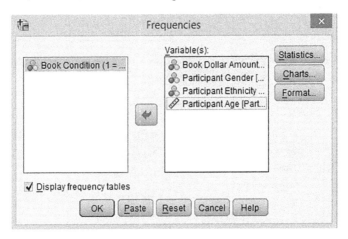

Now, click on Statistics and select the items I chose. You see that you have several options here, including the mean, median, mode, range, and standard deviation. You can even look at the minimum and maximum.

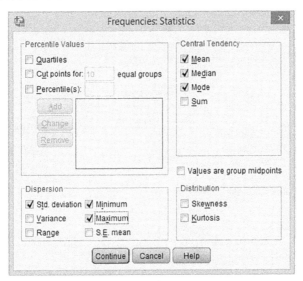

Now, click Continue and then OK to get to the output.

OUTPUT OF THE FREQUENCIES PROCEDURE IN SPSS

You will see several tables in your output, including one overall Statistics table followed by Frequency tables for each of the variables you added to the Variable(s) box.

Statistics

Statistics

		Book Dollar Amount	Participant Gender	Participant Ethnicity	Participant Age
N	Valid	20	20	20	20
	Missing	0	0	0	0
Mean		110.00	1.5500	2.0500	20.3500
Median		113.50	2.0000	2.0000	20.0000
Mode		134	2.00	1.00	18.00
Std. Deviation		32.859	.51042	1.05006	2.03328
Minimum		65	1.00	1.00	18.00
Maximum		164	2.00	4.00	24.00

Here you can see descriptive statistics for Book Dollar Amount, Participant Gender, Participant Ethnicity, and Participant Age. Once again, we see the mean Total information for Book Dollar Amount ($M = 110$, $SD = 32.86$), but it doesn't break it down by condition (High versus Low). We also see our descriptive information for age ($M = 20.35$, $SD = 2.03$), which duplicates the test we ran in the prior section. Finally, we have means and standard deviations (and other information) for gender and ethnicity. At this point I hope you're thinking, "Means and standard deviations for gender and ethnicity make no sense!" You're right—they don't. The only helpful columns in this Statistics table are Book Dollar Amount and Participant Age. So let's look at some other tables to get descriptive information about gender and ethnicity.

Frequency Table

Participant Gender

		Frequency	Percent	Valid Percent	Cumulative Percent
Valid	Male	9	45.0	45.0	45.0
	Female	11	55.0	55.0	100.0
	Total	20	100.0	100.0	

As the Participant Gender table shows, it appears to be a fairly even split here; there are 9 males and 11 females. Thus 45% are male and 55% are female. Between the statistics table and the frequency table, we can now write out our participant data. Now, consider ethnicity.

Participant Ethnicity

		Frequency	Percent	Valid Percent	Cumulative Percent
Valid	Caucasian	8	40.0	40.0	40.0
	African American	5	25.0	25.0	65.0
	Hispanic / Latino	5	25.0	25.0	90.0
	Asian	2	10.0	10.0	100.0
	Total	20	100.0	100.0	

We have eight Caucasians (40%), five African Americans (25%), five Hispanics/Latinos (25%), and two Asians (10%). In this table, there are zero Others, so that row is omitted. We now have enough information to write up our participant section in a journal-style methods section.

REPORTING THE OUTPUT FOR THE DESCRIPTIVES PROCEDURE

There were 20 participants in the study, including 9 men and 11 women, who ranged in age from 18 to 24 ($M = 20.35$, $SD = 2.03$). There were eight Caucasians (40%), five African Americans (25%), five Hispanics/Latinos (25%), and two Asians (10%).

Of course, you will see frequency tables for Book Dollar Amount and Participant Age as well. They look like this:

Book Dollar Amount

		Frequency	Percent	Valid Percent	Cumulative Percent
Valid	65	1	5.0	5.0	5.0
	68	1	5.0	5.0	10.0
	69	1	5.0	5.0	15.0
	73	1	5.0	5.0	20.0
	77	1	5.0	5.0	25.0
	86	1	5.0	5.0	30.0
	87	2	10.0	10.0	40.0
	88	1	5.0	5.0	45.0
	100	1	5.0	5.0	50.0
	127	1	5.0	5.0	55.0
	132	1	5.0	5.0	60.0
	133	1	5.0	5.0	65.0
	134	3	15.0	15.0	80.0
	135	1	5.0	5.0	85.0
	151	1	5.0	5.0	90.0
	156	1	5.0	5.0	95.0
	164	1	5.0	5.0	100.0
	Total	20	100.0	100.0	

Participant Age

		Frequency	Percent	Valid Percent	Cumulative Percent
Valid	18.00	5	25.0	25.0	25.0
	19.00	3	15.0	15.0	40.0
	20.00	3	15.0	15.0	55.0
	21.00	4	20.0	20.0	75.0
	22.00	1	5.0	5.0	80.0
	23.00	2	10.0	10.0	90.0
	24.00	2	10.0	10.0	100.0
	Total	20	100.0	100.0	

As you probably know, though, these tables don't provide as much help for interval or ratio data compared to tables that give us means and standard deviations.

Conclusion

Frequencies and Descriptives are the building blocks for future statistical tests. Make sure you can distinguish between nominal, ordinal, interval, and ratio scales as well as different measures of central tendency (mean, median, and mode).

To run tests yourself, download the Crash Course in Descriptive Statistics SPSS file at **study.sagepub.com/winter**.

Crash Course in Descriptive Statistics: Quiz Yourself!

(Answers in back of book)

Instructions: Imagine you ran frequencies to write out your participant data for a study. You inputted data into SPSS, which gave you the following output. Using these charts, answer the questions on the final page.

Statistics

		Participant Gender	Participant Ethnicity	Participant Age
N	Valid	144	144	143
	Missing	0	0	1
Mean		1.5069	2.0972	20.9930
Median		2.0000	2.0000	21.0000
Mode		2.00	2.00	22.00
Std. Deviation		.50170	1.01264	2.81719
Minimum		1.00	1.00	12.00
Maximum		2.00	6.00	29.00

(Continued)

(Continued)

Frequency Table

Participant Gender

		Frequency	Percent	Valid Percent	Cumulative Percent
Valid	Male	71	49.3	49.3	49.3
	Female	73	50.7	50.7	100.0
	Total	144	100.0	100.0	

Participant Ethnicity

		Frequency	Percent	Valid Percent	Cumulative Percent
Valid	Caucasian	22	15.3	15.3	15.3
	Hispanic	111	77.1	77.1	92.4
	African American	3	2.1	2.1	94.4
	Asian American	2	1.4	1.4	95.8
	Other	6	4.2	4.2	100.0
	Total	144	100.0	100.0	

Participant Age

		Frequency	Percent	Valid Percent	Cumulative Percent
Valid	12.00	3	2.1	2.1	2.1
	14.00	1	.7	.7	2.8
	15.00	3	2.1	2.1	4.9
	16.00	4	2.8	2.8	7.7
	17.00	1	.7	.7	8.4
	18.00	9	6.3	6.3	14.7
	19.00	13	9.0	9.1	23.8
	20.00	20	13.9	14.0	37.8
	21.00	22	15.3	15.4	53.1
	22.00	26	18.1	18.2	71.3
	23.00	19	13.2	13.3	84.6
	24.00	13	9.0	9.1	93.7
	25.00	4	2.8	2.8	96.5
	26.00	3	2.1	2.1	98.6
	27.00	1	.7	.7	99.3
	29.00	1	.7	.7	100.0
	Total	143	99.3	100.0	
Missing	System	1	.7		
Total		144	100.0		

1. Choose the correct range, mean, and standard deviation for participant age written in correct APA format.

   A. Participants ranged in age from 11 to 28 ($M = 20.99$, $SD = 2.82$).

   B. Participants ranged in age from 12 to 30 ($M = 20.99$, $SD = 2.82$).

    C. Participants ranged in age from 12 to 29 ($M = 20.99$, $SD = 2.82$).

    D. Participants ranged in age from 12 to 29 ($M = 2.82$, $SD = 20.99$).

    E. Participants ranged in age from 12 to 29 ($M = 20.99$, $SD = 22$).

2. Choose the correct frequency information for gender.

    A. There were 71 men (39%) and 73 women (61%).

    B. There were 71 men (49%) and 73 women (51%).

    C. There were 73 men (50%) and 71 women (50%).

    D. There were 71 men (51%) and 73 women (49%).

    E. There were 73 men (49%) and 71 women (51%).

3. Which of the following is the correct frequency information for ethnicity?

    A. In this sample, 21 participants were Caucasian (15%), 112 were Hispanic (77%), 3 were African American (2%), 3 were Asian (1%), and 6 did not provide their ethnicity (4%).

    B. In this sample, 22 participants were Caucasian (19%), 111 were Hispanic (67%), 3 were African American (4%), 2 were Asian (1%), and 3 did not provide their ethnicity (4%).

    C. In this sample, 20 participants were Caucasian (76%), 11 were Hispanic (21%), 3 were African American (2%), 6 were Asian (1%), and 6 did not provide their ethnicity (4%).

    D. In this sample, 22 participants were Caucasian (15%), 111 were Hispanic (77%), 3 were African American (2%), 2 were Asian (1%), and 6 did not provide their ethnicity (4%).

    E. In this sample, 15 participants were Caucasian (15%), 117 were Hispanic (77%), 3 were African American (2%), 2 were Asian (1%), and 6 did not provide their ethnicity (4%).

4. Which of the following scales was used for gender (nominal, ordinal, interval, or ratio)?

    A. Gender is a nominal variable.

    B. Gender is an ordinal variable.

    C. Gender is an interval variable.

    D. Gender is a ratio variable.

    E. None of the above.

(Continued)

(Continued)

5. For which (if any) of the three dependent variables in this data set (gender, age, ethnicity) would you report the standard deviation?

    A. Age, since it is measured on an interval scale

    B. Gender, since it is measured on an interval scale

    C. Ethnicity, since it is measured on an interval scale

    D. All of the above

    E. None of the above, since the standard deviation is inappropriate to use for all three variables

NONPARAMETRIC STATISTICS: CHI SQUARE

What follows is a quick reminder of nonparametric tests (focusing on the chi square). Quiz yourself on the chi square at the end of this chapter!

HOW, WHEN, AND WHY DO WE USE A *CHI SQUARE*?

The *chi square* is used to compare two or more levels of a categorical (nominal or ordinal) variable. I recommend looking at Chapter 1 (the crash course on descriptive statistics) for more information on interval and ratio scales, but I want to highlight nominal and ordinal scales here.

Nominal scales are based on assigning items to categories. For example, you can have yes versus no categories, or male versus female categories, or Honda versus Toyota versus Subaru versus Ford. For nominal scales, there is no better or worse/higher or lower—just different categories. (After all, which is higher: male or female?)

Ordinal scales have more order to them. That is, they are ranked. Thus there might be a better or worse ranking here (pizza is ranked highest, salad second highest, sandwiches third highest, haggis lowest for food preference). We might know the order, but we may not know how spread out those preferences are. That is, maybe pizza, salad, and sandwiches are all ranked very high in preference but haggis is ranked really, really low! Or think about a race. The first, second, and third place finishers may come in a few seconds apart while the fourth place finisher is over a minute behind.

For this crash course chapter, I want to focus only on the nominal scale. A chi square essentially looks at the percentage of cases that fall into categories of the variable. Let's say I look at gender as a variable in my study. I sample 200 people at random. There is a good chance I would get 100 men and 100 women, but I could also be off a little from this 50/50 ratio. That is, I could wind up with 95 men and 105 women just based on natural fluctuations of my data collection and selection procedure. The question then becomes: Are the observed differences in percentage of men/ women based on mere chance or something more significant? As another example, I might look to see if there are more guilty than not-guilty verdicts in a trial. If I poll jurors and find that 60% found guilt while 40% found no guilt, I might want to run a chi square to see if the difference is based on chance factors or something more.

Because we are looking at only two levels to our variable (men versus women and guilty versus not guilty), it is not appropriate to look at means and standard deviations. After all, what is a mean gender? No such thing, right? Thus we cannot use a *t*-test or ANOVA for this analysis, as those tests are based on mean scores (we'll cover those tests in Crash Course Chapters 3 and 4). The chi square, however, is designed to look at percentages and frequencies of data. There are different types of chi squares, though.

1. Chi Square—Goodness of Fit: In this test, we look at only one variable. Thus we can determine whether we have more men in our study than we should by chance, or we can see if there are more not-guilty verdicts than we should have by chance.

2. Chi Square—Test of Independence: For this test, we want to see if two variables are independent. Consider juror gender and verdict in the same chi square model. We might want to know if juror gender has an impact on verdict or whether verdict is independent of gender. Both variables here are nominal in nature (two levels to gender: male versus female; two levels to verdict: guilty versus not guilty).

The nice thing about chi squares is that there really are no assumptions about the shape of the distribution (we don't need a bell-shaped curve as we do for *t*-tests and ANOVAs). But the variables can't be on scales—just categories. Let's run this and interpret it in SPSS.

An Example: Social Influence and College Textbooks

Let's use the study we began in the chapter on descriptive statistics. A robust finding in social psychology is that when people have insufficient information about how to behave or what decision to make, they rely on others as a source of information. Imagine we ask college student participants how much money they spent on books last semester. We have them fill out their name and the amount of money they recall spending at the bottom of a book survey after the names and amounts listed by 10 prior participants. Unknown to our participants, we alter the amounts recalled by the 10 prior participants, creating one condition with a high average book price ($150) and one condition with a low average book price ($75). We predict that those who see high dollar amounts from prior participants will use that information as an anchor point and recall spending a similar high amount themselves. Those in our low dollar amount condition will anchor to that lower amount. We collect signatures and dollar amounts from 10 real participants randomly assigned to the High Dollar Condition and 10 real participants randomly assigned to the Low Dollar Condition. Consider the data.

High Dollar Condition ($)	Low Dollar Condition ($)
134	77
156	65
134	87
132	100
164	88
127	68
135	86
134	73
133	69
151	87
$\Sigma HD = 1,400$	$\Sigma LD = 800$
Mean = 140	Mean = 80
Standard Deviation = 12.33	Standard Deviation = 11.28

Eyeballing this, it looks like students recall spending more in the High Dollar Condition ($M = 140$, $SD = 12.33$) compared to students in the Low Dollar Condition ($M = 80$, $SD = 11.28$). But is this difference between $140 and $80 based simply on chance or something else? If it is based on chance, then I can say that both columns are pretty equal, and thus type of survey condition (high versus low) did not matter. If it is based on something other than chance, then I can conclude that there is something else at work here (probably the high or low dollar amounts provided by prior participants). We can look at this possibility using a *t*-test or other inferential statistical test that relies on the mean.

But suppose we wanted to see if participants paid attention to the manipulation. That is, we can ask them, "Did you think the prior participants who completed the book survey had a high or low estimation of the amount they spent on books?" Rather than an interval or ratio variable for Book Amount Recalled, we would have a nominal variable based on two responses: high estimate versus low estimate. We might see data like these:

High Dollar Condition (1 = High, 2 = Low)	Low Dollar Condition (1 = High, 2 = Low)
1	2
1	2
1	2
1	1
2	2
2	2
1	1
1	2
1	2
1	2

So eight participants in the High Dollar Condition recall high estimates from prior participants while only two participants in the Low Dollar Condition recall high estimates. Let's see how to run this in SPSS. Since this example involves two different variables (high/low condition and high/low estimates), we will run a chi square test of independence.

SPSS: OUR BOOK STUDY

1. Click Analyze > Descriptive Statistics > Crosstabs . . . on the top menu as shown in the following screenshot.

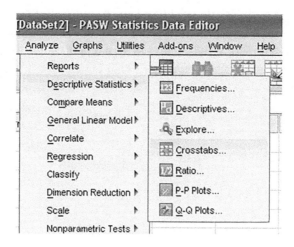

You will be presented with the following:

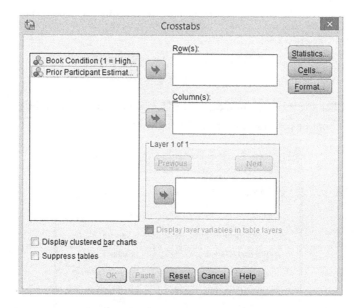

Transfer one of the variables into the Row(s) box and the other variable into the Column(s) box. In our example we will transfer the Book Condition variable into the Row(s) box and Prior Participant Estimate into the Column(s) box. There are two ways to do this. You can highlight the variable with your mouse and then use the ▸ button to transfer the variables, or you can drag and drop the variables. How do you know which variable goes in which box? There is no right or wrong way. It will depend on how you want to present your data.

If you want to display clustered bar charts (recommended), then make sure that "Display clustered bar charts" is ticked.

You will end up with a screen similar to the one in the following screenshot.

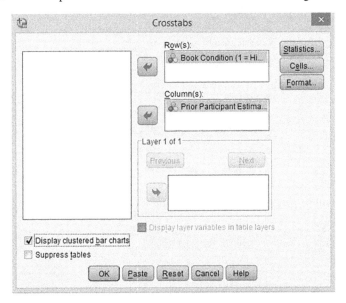

1. Click the [Statistics...] button. Select the "Chi-square" and "Phi and Cramer's V" options as shown in the following screenshot.

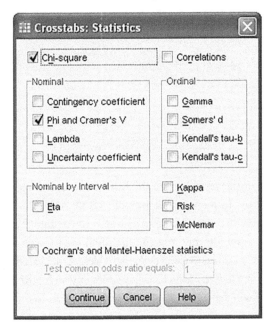

Click the [Continue] button.

2. Click the [Cells...] button. Select "Observed" from the Counts area and "Row" from the Percentages area as shown in the following screenshot.

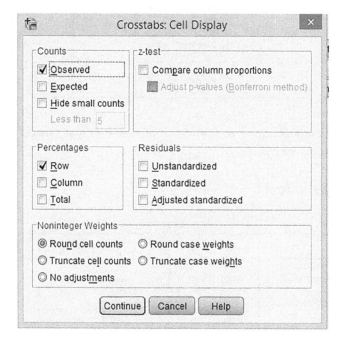

3. Click the [OK] button to generate your output.

OUTPUT OF THE INDEPENDENT CHI SQUARE IN SPSS

You will see several tables for the chi square, but ignore the case processing table.

Book Condition (1 = High, 2 = Low) * Prior Participant Estimate (1 = High, 2 = Low) Crosstabulation

The nice thing about this table is it tells you exactly what you ran in the name of the table!

As you can see, eight participants in the High Condition thought the Prior Participant Estimates were high (two thought they were low). Alternatively, two participants in the Low Condition thought Prior Participant Estimates were

Book Condition (1 = High, 2 - Low) * Prior Participant Estimate (1 = High, 2 = Low) Crosstabulation

			Prior Participant Estimate (1 = High, 2 = Low)		
			High	Low	Total
Book Condition (1 = High, 2 - Low)	High	Count	8	2	10
		% within Book Condition (1 = High, 2 - Low)	80.0%	20.0%	100.0%
	Low	Count	2	8	10
		% within Book Condition (1 = High, 2 - Low)	20.0%	80.0%	100.0%
Total		Count	10	10	20
		% within Book Condition (1 = High, 2 - Low)	50.0%	50.0%	100.0%

high (eight thought they were low). But is this statistically significant? For that, we look to the next table.

Chi-Square Tests

Chi-Square Tests

	Value	df	Asymp. Sig. (2-sided)	Exact Sig. (2-sided)	Exact Sig. (1-sided)
Pearson Chi-Square	7.200[a]	1	.007		
Continuity Correction[b]	5.000	1	.025		
Likelihood Ratio	7.710	1	.005		
Fisher's Exact Test				.023	.012
Linear-by-Linear Association	6.840	1	.009		
N of Valid Cases	20				

a. 0 cells (0.0%) have expected count less than 5. The minimum expected count is 5.00.

b. Computed only for a 2x2 table

Focus on the Pearson Chi-Square row. Based on this row, we can see that the chi square is significant, $\chi^2(1) = 7.20$, $p = .007$.

Symmetric Measures

Our final table looks at symmetric measures, or basically the degree of association among the factors in the analysis (how correlated are they?). As you can see in the following table, both Phi and Cramer's V are very high (.600 on a 0 to +1 scale, which makes .600 pretty high). Both are significant at $p = .007$. Phi is appropriate when you use a 2×2 design (two factors with two levels each, as we did here with two Prior Participant Estimates (High versus Low) and two Book Dollar Amount Conditions (High versus Low). Cramer's V is useful when one factor has more levels than the other.

Symmetric Measures

		Value	Approx. Sig.
Nominal by Nominal	Phi	.600	.007
	Cramer's V	.600	.007
N of Valid Cases		20	

a. Not assuming the null hypothesis.

b. Using the asymptotic standard error assuming the null hypothesis.

INTERPRETING THE INDEPENDENT CHI SQUARE IN SPSS

If nonsignificant, the write-up for the chi square is relatively easy. You simply write:

A chi square test of independence was calculated comparing whether participants given High versus Low book survey saw Prior Participant Estimates as high or low. No significant relationship was found, $\chi^2(1) = 1.27, p > .05$, and phi did not show a significant effect.

However, if a significant result occurs (as it did in our study), the write-up looks like this:

A chi square test of independence was calculated comparing whether participants given a High versus Low book survey condition saw Prior Participant Estimates as high or low. A significant relationship emerged, $\chi^2(1) = 7.20, p = .007$. Most participants in the High Dollar Condition recalled Prior Participants making high estimates (80%), while most participants in the Low Dollar Condition recalled Prior Participants making low estimates (80%). Phi showed a large effect.

ANOTHER QUICK EXAMPLE: THREE LEVELS TO YOUR MAIN INDEPENDENT VARIABLE

Now, assume that we had three levels to our book survey study: High, Low, and Medium (that is, they see a dollar amount between the high and low extremes).

If we still have Prior Participant Estimates as a dichotomized dependent variable (High versus Low), we can still run our chi square. Imagine that five of our Medium participants think Prior Participant Estimates were high and five think the estimates were low. Consider our SPSS output in the following tables. For the data in these tables, we have the following interpretation:

> A chi square test of independence was calculated comparing whether participants given the High versus Medium versus Low book survey saw Prior Participant Estimates as high or low. A significant relationship emerged, $\chi^2(2) = 7.20$, $p = .027$. Most participants in the High Dollar Condition recalled Prior Participants making high estimates (80%), most participants in the Low Dollar Condition recalled Prior Participants making low estimates (80%), but participants were split in the Medium Dollar Condition, with half (50%) recalling Prior Participants making high estimates. Cramer's V showed a significant effect.

Here, our degrees of freedom, or *df*, changed a bit (we now have three conditions, so $k - 1 = 2$, or 3 groups minus 1 equals 2). If we had two groups, our *df* would be 1 ($k - 1 = 1$, or $2 - 1 = 1$), while four groups would give us a *df* of 3.

Book Condition (1 = High, 2 - Low, 3 = Medium) ' Prior Participant Estimate (1 = High, 2 = Low) Crosstabulation

| | | | | Prior Participant Estimate (1 = High, 2 = Low) | | |
				High	Low	Total
Book Condition (1 = High, 2 - Low, 3 = Medium)	High	Count		8	2	10
		% within Book Condition (1 = High, 2 - Low, 3 = Medium)		80.0%	20.0%	100.0%
	Low	Count		2	8	10
		% within Book Condition (1 = High, 2 - Low, 3 = Medium)		20.0%	80.0%	100.0%
	Medium	Count		5	5	10
		% within Book Condition (1 = High, 2 - Low, 3 = Medium)		50.0%	50.0%	100.0%
Total		Count		15	15	30
		% within Book Condition (1 = High, 2 - Low, 3 = Medium)		50.0%	50.0%	100.0%

Chi-Square Tests

	Value	df	Asymp. Sig. (2-sided)
Pearson Chi-Square	7.200[a]	2	.027
Likelihood Ratio	7.710	2	.021
Linear-by-Linear Association	1.740	1	.187
N of Valid Cases	30		

a. 0 cells (0.0%) have expected count less than 5. The minimum expected count is 5.00.

Symmetric Measures

		Value	Approx. Sig.
Nominal by Nominal	Phi	.490	.027
	Cramer's V	.490	.027
N of Valid Cases		30	

a. Not assuming the null hypothesis.

b. Using the asymptotic standard error assuming the null hypothesis.

If you want to run these tests yourself, download the Crash Course in Nonparametric Statistics SPSS file from the website at **study.sagepub.com/winter**. There is a separate file for the 2 × 2 chi square and the 3 × 2 chi square.

Crash Course in Nonparametric Statistics: Quiz Yourself!

Instructions: Imagine you randomly assign participants to an IV Task where they complete either an easy anagram solving task ("Please rearrange the letters BAT to form a new word." This is very easy, as it can be rearranged to TAB.) or an impossible-to-solve hard anagram task ("Please rearrange the letters ORANGE to form a new word." This task this cannot actually be done!). You then ask all participants to solve a second anagram by rearranging CINERAMA to form a new word. This, of course, is difficult, but it can be rearranged to AMERICAN. Based on the theory of learned helplessness (in which prior failures make it less likely for people to try hard on future tasks), you believe those given an easy first anagram to solve (TAB) will solve the anagram CINERAMA, and those who get the hard first anagram (ORANGE) will not solve the anagram CINERAMA.

1. What is the independent variable in this study?

   A. Level of frustration

   B. Whether they can rearrange the word CINERAMA

   C. Whether they can rearrange both the words BAT and ORANGE

   D. Which problem-solving task they received (easy BAT anagram versus impossible-to-solve ORANGE anagram)

   E. There is too little information in this study to determine the independent variable

2. What is the dependent variable in this study?

   A. Level of frustration

   B. Whether they can rearrange the word CINERAMA

(Continued)

(Continued)

   C. Whether they can rearrange both the words BAT and ORANGE

   D. Which problem-solving task they received (easy BAT anagram versus impossible-to-solve ORANGE anagram)

   E. There is too little information in this study to determine the dependent variable

You run a chi square on this data set and get the following SPSS output. Using this output, interpret the information.

Case Processing Summary

	Cases					
	Valid		Missing		Total	
	N	Percent	N	Percent	N	Percent
IV Task * Anagram Solved	61	100.0%	0	0.0%	61	100.0%

IV Task * Anagram Solved Crosstabulation

			Anagram Solved		Total
			Yes	No	
IV Task	Easy	Count	26	4	30
		% within IV Task	86.7%	13.3%	100.0%
	Hard	Count	6	25	31
		% within IV Task	19.4%	80.6%	100.0%
Total		Count	32	29	61
		% within IV Task	52.5%	47.5%	100.0%

Chi-Square Tests

	Value	df	Asymp. Sig. (2-sided)	Exact Sig. (2-sided)	Exact Sig. (1-sided)
Pearson Chi-Square	27.698[a]	1	.000		
Continuity Correction[b]	25.065	1	.000		
Likelihood Ratio	30.394	1	.000		
Fisher's Exact Test				.000	.000
Linear-by-Linear Association	27.244	1	.000		
N of Valid Cases	61				

a. 0 cells (0.0%) have expected count less than 5. The minimum expected count is 14.26.
b. Computed only for a 2x2 table

Symmetric Measures

		Value	Approx. Sig.
Nominal by Nominal	Phi	.674	.000
	Cramer's V	.674	.000
N of Valid Cases		61	

a. Not assuming the null hypothesis.
b. Using the asymptotic standard error assuming the null hypothesis.

3. How many participants in the hard anagram condition solved the CINERAMA anagram?

   A. Only 29 participants solved the CINERAMA anagram in the hard condition. You can contrast this with 32 participants who solved it in the easy condition.

   B. Only 32 participants solved the CINERAMA anagram in the hard condition. You can contrast this with 29 participants who solved it in the easy condition.

   C. Only six participants solved the CINERAMA anagram in the hard condition. You can contrast this with 26 participants who solved it in the easy condition.

   D. Only 26 participants solved the CINERAMA anagram in the hard condition. You can contrast this with six participants who solved it in the easy condition.

   E. Only six participants solved the CINERAMA anagram in the hard condition. You can contrast this with 29 participants who solved it in the easy condition.

4. What is the main difference between a chi square goodness of fit and a chi square test of independence?

   A. For a goodness of fit test we look at more than one variable, while we look at only one variable for a test of independence.

   B. For a goodness of fit test we look at only one variable, while we look at more than one variable for a test of independence.

   C. For a goodness of fit test we use interval scales, while we look ratio scales for a test of independence.

   D. For a goodness of fit test we need to have a normal curve, while a test of independence does not need a normal curve.

   E. There is no difference between a chi square goodness of fit and a chi square test of independence. They are synonymous.

5. Finally, which of the following represents the correct way to write out the results for this chi square in an APA-formatted results section?

   A. A chi square test of independence was calculated comparing whether participants solved or did not solve an anagram (CINERAMA). A significant relationship emerged, $\chi^2(2) = 27.70$, $p < .001$. Most participants in the easy anagram condition solved the CINERAMA anagram (86.7%), while very few participants in the hard anagram condition solved the CINERAMA anagram (19.4%). Phi showed a significant effect.

   B. A chi square test of independence was calculated comparing whether participants solved or did not solve an anagram (CINERAMA). A significant relationship failed to emerge, $\chi^2(2) = 27.70$, $p > .05$. Participants in the easy anagram condition solved the CINERAMA anagram (86.7%) at the same rate as participants in the hard anagram condition solved the CINERAMA anagram (81.6%). Phi showed a significant effect.

(Continued)

(Continued)

C. A chi square test of independence was calculated comparing whether participants solved or did not solve an anagram (CINERAMA). A significant relationship failed to emerge, $\chi^2(1) = 0.67$, $p > .05$. Participants in the easy anagram condition solved the CINERAMA anagram (86.7%) at the same rate as participants in the hard anagram condition (81.6%). Phi showed a significant effect.

D. A chi square test of independence was calculated comparing whether participants solved or did not solve an anagram (CINERAMA). A significant relationship emerged, $\chi^2(1) = 27.70$, $p < .001$. Most participants in the easy anagram condition solved the CINERAMA anagram (86.7%), while very few participants in the hard anagram condition solved the CINERAMA anagram (19.4%). Phi showed a large effect.

E. A chi square test of independence was calculated comparing whether participants solved or did not solve an anagram (CINERAMA). A significant relationship emerged, $\chi^2(1) = 27.70$, $p < .001$. Few participants in the easy anagram condition solved the CINERAMA anagram (19.4%), while most participants in the hard anagram condition solved the CINERAMA anagram (86.7%). Phi showed a significant effect.

THE *t*-TEST

What follows is a quick reminder of inferential statistics (focusing on the *t*-test). Quiz yourself on the *t*-test at the end of this chapter!

HOW, WHEN, AND WHY DO A *t*-TEST?

Let me give you some basic information about the *t*-test. The *t*-test is used to compare two means to see if they differ significantly from one another. In this analysis, we need two pieces of information: the means for each group and the *t*-test information itself.

Do you recall what a mean is? It is the average score. That is, you add up all of the scores and divide by the number of total scores to arrive at the average. Since a *t*-test looks at two different conditions, this means you have two means: one for each condition. The means here (and the standard deviation) are *descriptive statistics*. That is, they help *describe* the data.

The *t*-test information itself is a test of *inferential statistics*. That is, we *infer* significant differences between the two groups. When writing it out, you will see a very common layout for the *t*-test, something like: $t(14) = 2.61$, $p = .021$. The *t* tells us this is a *t*-test. The 14 tells us our degrees of freedom. The 2.61 is the actual number for the *t*-test. The *p* indicates whether it is significant (if it is less than .05, then it is significant).

We run a *t*-test only under certain conditions.

First, our dependent variable (the variable we measure) must be continuous/scaled. That is, the DV has to be along a scale. For example, it can be an attitude ("On a scale of 1 to 9, how angry are you?") or a time frame ("How quickly did the salesperson help the customer on a scale of zero seconds to a thousand seconds?"). We call these interval or ratio scales. We *cannot* run a *t*-test on categorical data. That is, if we have a yes/no question ("Are you lonely: Yes or No") or a category-based question ("What is your favorite food: hamburgers, pizza, salad, or tacos?"), then we cannot run a *t*-test. These latter questions are based more on choice of option rather than an actual rating scale, and thus we cannot use a *t*-test on them.

Second, we run a *t*-test when we have two conditions to compare. For example, we compare the mean from Condition A to the mean from Condition B. If our *t*-test is significant ($p < .05$), then we simply see which mean is higher. "The *t*-Test was significant, $t(13) = 2.51$, $p = .023$, with Condition A (mean = 42.23) less than Condition B (mean = 62.29)."

An Example: Social Influence and College Textbooks

Let's use the study we began in the chapter on descriptive statistics. A robust finding in social psychology is that when people have insufficient information about how to behave or what decision to make, they rely on others as a source of information. Imagine we ask college student participants how much money they spent on books last semester. We have them fill out their name and the amount of money they recall spending at the bottom of a book survey after the names and amounts listed by 10 prior participants. Unknown to our participants, we alter the amounts recalled by the 10 prior participants, creating one condition with a high average book price ($150) and one condition with a low average book price ($75). We predict that those who see high dollar amounts from prior participants will use that information as an anchor point and recall spending a similar high amount themselves. Those in our low dollar amount condition will anchor to that lower amount. We collect signatures and dollar amounts from 10 real participants randomly assigned to the High Dollar (HD) condition and 10 real participants randomly assigned to the Low Dollar (LD) condition. Consider the data:

High Dollar Condition ($)	Low Dollar Condition ($)
134	77
156	65
134	87
132	100
164	88
127	68
135	86
134	73
133	69
151	87
$\Sigma HD = 1,400$	$\Sigma LD = 800$
Mean = 140	*Mean* = 80
Standard Deviation = 12.33	*Standard Deviation* = 11.28

Recall that Σ, or the symbol for sigma, means "the sum of." Thus Σ_{HD} is the sum of the scores for the High Dollar Condition. That is, $134 + 156 + 134 + 132 + 164 + 127 + 135 + 134 + 133 + 151 = 1,400$. There are 10 scores here, so we divide $1,400 / 10 = 140$, giving us our mean of $140. We do the same thing for the Low Dollar Condition, which results in a mean of $80. But is this difference between $140 and $80 based simply on chance or something else? If it is based on chance, then we can say that both columns are pretty equal, and thus type of high versus low survey conditions did not matter. If it is based on something other than chance, then we can conclude that there is something else at work here (probably the high or low dollar amounts provided by prior participants). We can look at this possibility using a *t*-test or other inferential statistical test that relies on the mean.

For the first part of our analysis, we compare the means. As you see, $140 in the High Dollar Condition seems a lot higher than $80 in the Low Dollar Condition. Thus the means seem to support our prediction, but we are not done yet. Just because the means *seem* to differ doesn't mean they *do* differ. To make that assessment, we run the *t*-test and look at the *p* value to see if it is $p < .05$. We can do this by hand (which I encourage) or we can take the easy road and let SPSS calculate it for us. I am going to take the easy road, but keep in mind that we still have to interpret what SPSS tells us.

For the next section, I am going to open SPSS and run an independent samples *t*-test. I'll use screenshots from SPSS as I go, but feel free to run these analyses yourself. Just set up your SPSS file like mine (or download the Crash Course in Inferential Statistics: The *t*-Test SPSS file from the book's website at **study .sagepub.com/winter**). I am just going to give you the basics here, but you can refer to other sources to figure out some of the information we get from the *t*-test that is not fully covered in this chapter (e.g., Levene's test, normality testing).

SPSS: OUR BOOK SURVEY STUDY

1. Click Analyze > Compare Means > Independent-Samples T Test . . . on the top menu as shown in the following screenshot.

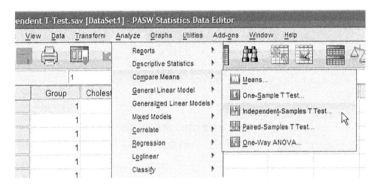

You will be presented with the following:

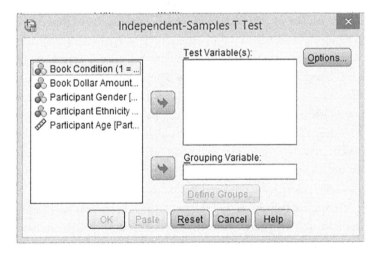

2. Our first task is to place our dependent variable in the Test Variable(s)
    box and our independent variable in the Grouping Variable(s) box by
    highlighting the relevant variables and clicking the ■ button. Note
    that SPSS uses different names for variables. It calls the dependent
    variable the Test Variable(s), and it calls the independent variable the
    Grouping Variable. Just remember that our DV (the test variable)
    must be scaled in order to run this test (1 to 9, or 1 to 5, or even
    0 to 100,000), while the IV has to be categorical (yes vs. no, men
    vs. women, old vs. young, Republican vs. Democrat, high vs. low,
    etc.). For now, let's use Book Dollar Amount as our Test Variable
    (our dependent variable) and IVBook$Condition (our independent
    variable, which is the same thing as our Book Condition, just with a
    slightly different name).

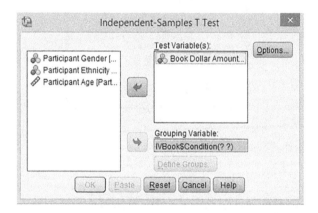

3. You then need to define the groups (IV Condition). Click the ▣ Define Groups…
    button.

You will be presented with the following screen:

4. Enter **1** into the Group 1 box and enter **2** into the Group 2 box. Want to know why we do this? Well, remember that we labeled the High condition as **1** and the Low condition as **2**? That's why we use 1 and 2. NOTE: If you have more than two groups (e.g., a Medium [3] group, or a neutral group with No Prior Names on the survey [4]), or even a group 5, 6, or 7!), you could type 1 into the Group 1 box and 3 into the Group 2 box to compare the High condition with the Medium condition. Since we have only two groups here, we will stick with 1 and 2.

5. Click the [Continue] button

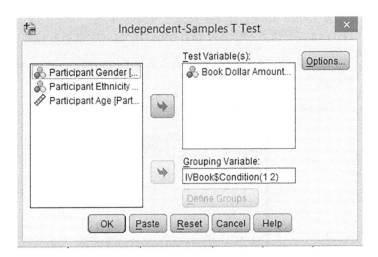

6. Click OK.

OUTPUT OF THE INDEPENDENT *t*-TEST IN SPSS

You will be presented with two tables containing all the data generated by the Independent *t*-test procedure in SPSS.

Group Statistics Table (or Descriptive Statistics)

This table provides useful descriptive statistics for the two groups that you compared, including the mean and standard deviation. Remember, these *describe* the data for us.

Group Statistics

	Book Condition (1 = High, 2 - Low)	N	Mean	Std. Deviation	Std. Error Mean
Book Dollar Amount	High	10	140.00	12.329	3.899
	Low	10	80.00	11.284	3.568

As you can see, we have 10 participants in the High Condition and 10 participants in the Low Condition. The mean for the High Condition is 140 (*SD* = 12.33) and the mean for the Low Condition is 80 (*SD* = 11.28). We can ignore the Std. Error Mean for now, but we will need the rest of the information in our write-up, so we'll come back to this table.

Independent Samples Test Table

This table provides the independent *t*-test results and Levene's Test for Equality of Variances.

Independent Samples Test

		Levene's Test for Equality of Variances		t-test for Equality of Means					95% Confidence Interval of the Difference	
		F	Sig.	t	df	Sig. (2-tailed)	Mean Difference	Std. Error Difference	Lower	Upper
Book Dollar Amount	Equal variances assumed	.059	.811	11.352	18	.000	60.000	5.285	48.896	71.104
	Equal variances not assumed			11.352	17.861	.000	60.000	5.285	48.890	71.110

Levene's test looks at the variances between the two groups. If significant, this means that the groups differ in their variance within each group, violating some of the *t*-test assumptions. We don't actually want this to be significant. If it is, it means that the groups vary based on something other than the independent variable. Given that the *t*-test is robust, it may not make any difference, but we would simply use the bottom row (Equal variances not assumed) when Levene is significant. Since our Levene's test *p* value is .811, it is not significant, which means we'll use the top row. Let's ignore Levene and focus on the more important features of the table. I'll remove several unneeded columns.

Independent Samples Test

		t-test for Equality of Means		
		t	df	Sig. (2-tailed)
Book Dollar Amount	Equal variances assumed	11.352	18	.000
	Equal variances not assumed	11.352	17.861	.000

The Independent Samples Test table contains the important information we will need for our *t*-test (outlined in the dashed box; you can match the *t*-test info in the dashed box with the *t*-test write-up in the text below). We will use the Equal variances assumed row. The two groups do differ, with a *t*-value of 11.35, a *df* of 18, and a *p* value less than .001. We write it up as $t(18) = 11.35, p < .001$.

For a journal-style write-up, we are going to need both of our tables—the descriptive table (with our means and standard deviations) and the independent samples *t*-test table. I've once again included the descriptives table (the "group statistics"). The important info is in the dash box.

Group Statistics

	Book Condition (1 = High, 2 - Low)	N	Mean	Std. Deviation	Std. Error Mean
Book Dollar Amount	High	10	140.00	12.329	3.899
	Low	10	80.00	11.284	3.568

REPORTING THE OUTPUT OF THE INDEPENDENT *t*-TEST

We report the statistics in this format: *t*(degrees of freedom[*df*]) = *t*-value, *p* = significance level. In our case this would be: $t(18) = 11.35, p < 0.001$, and our means and SDs would be ($M = 140, SD = 12.33$) for the High Condition and

(M = **80**, SD = **11.28**) for the Low Condition. We would report the results of the study as follows:

> We ran an independent samples t-test with book condition as our independent variable and amount spent on books as our dependent variable. The t-test was significant, $t(18) = 11.35$, $p < .001$. Participants in the high book condition ($M = 140$, $SD = 12.33$) recalled spending more money on books than participants in the low book condition ($M = 80$, $SD = 11.28$).

That's it! Not too hard, right? Just remember the basics here: We use a t-test to look at the differences between two means to see if the means differ significantly. We need two SPSS tables to make this assessment: the descriptive statistics tables ("group statistics") and the t-test table ("Independent Samples t-Test").

You might have noticed some demographic data in the file. Analyze and write up descriptive statistics for the sample on your own!

Crash Course in Inferential Statistics (The t-Test): Quiz Yourself!

Instructions: Imagine you randomly assign participants to complete either a hard anagram-solving task ("Please rearrange the letters CINERAMA to form a new word." This, of course, is difficult but not impossible, as it can be rearranged to AMERICAN.) versus an easy anagram solving task ("Please rearrange the letters BAT to form a new word." This is very easy, as it can be rearranged to TAB.). You then measure participants' levels of frustration in completing the anagram solving task on a scale ranging from 1 (very frustrating) to 9 (not at all frustrating). Using these charts, answer the following questions.

1. What is the independent variable in this study?

    A. Level of frustration

    B. Whether they can rearrange the word CINERAMA

    C. Whether they can rearrange the word BAT

    D. Which problem-solving task they received (hard versus easy anagram)

    E. There is too little information in this study to determine the independent variable.

(Continued)

(Continued)

2. What is the dependent variable in this study?

    A. Level of frustration

    B. Whether they can rearrange the word CINERAMA

    C. Whether they can rearrange the word BAT

    D. Which problem-solving task they received (hard versus easy anagram)

    E. There is too little information in this study to determine the dependent variable.

You run a *t*-test on this data set and get the following SPSS output. Using this output, interpret the information.

Group Statistics

	IV Task	N	Mean	Std. Deviation	Std. Error Mean
Frustrating	Easy	30	8.3667	1.29943	.23724
	Hard	31	1.3871	.49514	.08893

Independent Samples Test

		Levene's Test for Equality of Variances		t-test for Equality of Means		
		F	Sig.	t	df	Sig. (2-tailed)
Frustrating	Equal variances assumed	1.571	.215	27.893	59	.000
	Equal variances not assumed			27.548	37.016	.000

3. Choose the correct means and standard deviations for the easy and hard conditions.

    A. The easy condition has a mean of 1.39 and standard deviation of 0.50, while the hard condition has a mean of 8.37 and a standard deviation of 1.30.

    B. The easy condition has a mean of 8.37 and standard deviation of .050, while the hard condition has a mean of 1.39 and a standard deviation of 1.30.

    C. The easy condition has a mean of 1.57 and standard deviation of 0.24, while the hard condition has a mean of 37.02 and a standard deviation of 0.09.

    D. The easy condition has a mean of 27.89 and standard deviation of 59, while the hard condition has a mean of 27.55 and a standard deviation of 37.02.

    E. The easy condition has a mean of 8.37 and standard deviation of 1.30, while the hard condition has a mean of 1.39 and a standard deviation of 0.50.

4. Is the *t*-test significant, and how would you write that out in APA format?

    A. Yes, the *t*-test is significant, $t(27.89) = 59$, $p < .001$.

    B. Yes, the *t*-test is significant, $t(59) = 27.89$, $p < .001$.

    C. No, the *t*-test is not significant, $t(27.89) = 59$, $p > .001$.

    D. No, the *t*-test is not significant, $t(59) = 27.89$, $p > .001$.

    E. It is impossible to tell from this data set if the *t*-test is significant.

5. Finally, which of the following shows the correct results as you would write them in an APA-formatted results section?

    A. We ran an independent samples *t*-test with anagram condition as our independent variable and frustration as our dependent variable. The *t*-test was significant, $t(59) = 27.89$, $p < .001$. Participants were more frustrated in the hard anagram condition ($M = 8.37$, $SD = 1.30$) than the easy anagram condition ($M = 1.39$, $SD = 0.50$).

    B. We ran an independent samples *t*-test with anagram condition as our independent variable and frustration as our dependent variable. The *t*-test was not significant, $t(59) = 27.89$, $p > .05$. Participants were no more frustrated in the hard anagram condition ($M = 1.39$, $SD = 0.50$) than the easy anagram condition ($M = 8.37$, $SD = 1.30$).

    C. We ran an independent samples *t*-test with anagram condition as our independent variable and frustration as our dependent variable. The *t*-test was significant, $t(59) = 27.89$, $p < .001$. Participants were more frustrated in the hard anagram condition ($M = 1.39$, $SD = 0.50$) than the easy anagram condition ($M = 8.37$, $SD = 1.30$).

    D. We ran an independent samples *t*-test with anagram condition as our independent variable and frustration as our dependent variable. The *t*-test was not significant, $t(27.89) = 59$, $p > .05$. Participants were no more frustrated in the hard anagram condition ($M = 1.39$, $SD = 0.50$) than the easy anagram condition ($M = 8.37$, $SD = 1.30$).

    E. We ran an independent samples *t*-test with anagram condition as our independent variable and frustration as our dependent variable. The *t*-test was significant, $t(27.89) = 59$, $p < .001$. Participants were more frustrated in the hard anagram condition ($M = 1.39$, $SD = 0.50$) than the easy anagram condition ($M = 8.37$, $SD = 1.30$).

THE ONE-WAY
(SIMPLE) ANOVA

What follows is a quick reminder of inferential statistics (focusing on the one-way ANOVA, or the simple ANOVA). Quiz yourself on the one-way ANOVA at the end of this chapter!

HOW, WHEN, AND
WHY DO A ONE-WAY ANOVA?

Do you recall the *t*-test, where we compared two means to see whether and in what direction the means differed? Well, a one-way ANOVA is very similar, but here we compare three or more means to see if they differ significantly from one another. The name *one-way* implies one independent variable in this design, though this one independent variable can have three or more levels. In this analysis, we need three pieces of information: (1) the means for each of the three groups (descriptive statistics), (2) the one-way ANOVA information itself, and (3) post hoc tests.

1. Once again, remember that a *mean* is the average score for that condition. That is, you add up all of the scores in a condition and divide by the number of total scores to arrive at the average. Since a one-way ANOVA looks at three or more different conditions, we have at least three means: one for each condition. The means here (plus the standard deviation) are *descriptive statistics*. That is, they help *describe* the data.

2. The one-way ANOVA information itself is a test of *inferential statistics*. That is, we *infer* significant differences between the three or more groups. When writing it out, you will see a very common layout for the one-way ANOVA, something like this: $F(2, 134) = 2.61, p = .021$. The F tells you this is a one-way ANOVA. The 2 and 134 tell us our degrees of freedom. The 2.61 is the actual number for the one-way ANOVA. The p indicates whether it is significant (if it is less than .05, then it is significant).

3. Finally, we have to consider post hoc tests. You might recall using the Tukey post hoc test in the past, but do you remember why you used it? Take a step back and think about the *t*-test, which looked at two means: Mean A and Mean B. If Mean A is 4.56 and Mean B is 7.67 and your *t*-test is significant (that is, p is less than .05), then you simply compare the two means to see which is higher: Mean A or Mean B. Here, Mean B is clearly higher (7.67 is higher than 4.56, and since the *t*-test is significant then Mean B is significantly higher than Mean A). But when we have three levels to our independent variable, we are now dealing with three means: Mean A, Mean B, and Mean C. Let's say Mean A is 4.56, Mean B is 7.67, and Mean C is 6.21. If our one-way ANOVA is significant (that is, it is less than .05), we know the means differ. The question is, *which* of the three means differ? Does Mean A differ from Mean B? Does Mean B differ from Mean C? Does Mean A differ from Mean C? Or there might be other combinations. Maybe Mean A and Mean C do not differ from each other, but both are significantly lower than Mean B. Unlike the *t*-test, we don't know which of the three means differ, which is why we run a post hoc test (like Tukey) to compare Mean A to Mean B, and Mean A to Mean C, and Mean B to Mean C. It runs all of those analyses for us in one test. So you might wonder, "Why not just run three *t*-tests, with one *t*-test comparing Mean A to Mean B, a second *t*-test comparing Mean B to Mean C, and a third *t*-test comparing Mean B to Mean C?" Well, you could actually do that, but we run into a Type I error. That is, the more tests we run, the greater the chance one of them will be significant, even if there is no actual significant difference between conditions. That is, if we run three *t*-tests, we open up the chance of one of them being falsely positive. With the one-way ANOVA, we just run the one test to compare the three means (note that the post hoc tests are still part of the one-way ANOVA—it compares the three means under the umbrella of the one-way ANOVA test).

As with the *t*-test, we run a one-way ANOVA only under certain conditions.

First, our dependent variable (the variable we measure) must be continuous/ scaled. That is, the DV has to be along a scale. For example, it can be an attitude ("On a scale of 1 to 9, how angry are you?") or a time frame ("How quickly did the salesperson help the customer on a scale of zero seconds to a thousand seconds?"). We call these interval or ratio scales. We *cannot* run a one-way ANOVA on categorical data. That is, if we have a yes/no question ("Are you lonely: yes or no") or a category-based question ("What is your favorite food: hamburgers, pizza, salad, or tacos?"), then we cannot run a one-way ANOVA. These latter questions are based more on choice of option rather than an actual rating scale, and thus we cannot use a one-way ANOVA on them.

Second, we run a one-way ANOVA when we have only one independent variable and that independent variable has at least three conditions (Note: it can have more than three levels, but you still have only one independent variable). That is, we compare the means from Condition A, Condition B, and Condition C (and possible Condition D, Condition E, etc.). If our one-way ANOVA is significant ($p < .05$), then we look at our post hoc tests to see which means differ. "The one-way ANOVA was significant, $F(2, 134) = 2.61$, $p = .021$. Tukey post hoc tests showed that Condition A (mean = 140) was significantly lower than Condition B (mean = 80). In addition, Condition C (mean = 120) was significantly higher than Condition B. However, Condition A did not differ significantly from Condition C."

Let's see how this looks using the example we've used in prior crash course quizzes: the book survey study.

An Example: Social Influence and College Textbooks

Let's use the study we began in the chapter on descriptive statistics. A robust finding in social psychology is that when people have insufficient information about how to behave or what decision to make, they rely on others as a source of information. Imagine we ask college student participants how much money they spent on books last semester. We have them fill out their name and the amount of money they recall spending at the bottom of a book survey after the names and amounts listed by 10 prior participants. Unknown to our participants, we alter the amounts recalled by the 10 prior participants, creating one condition with a high average book price ($150) and one condition with a low average book price

($75). But here we add in a third condition, a control group where participants do not see any prior participant data. We predict that those who see high dollar amounts from prior participants will use that information as an anchor point and recall spending a similar high amount themselves. Those in our low dollar amount condition will anchor to that lower amount. We think that those in our control condition will recall spending an amount between the high and low conditions. We collect signatures and dollar amounts from 10 real participants randomly assigned to the High Dollar Condition, 10 real participants randomly assigned to the Low Dollar Condition, and 10 real participants randomly assigned to the Control Dollar Condition. Their data are as follows.

High Dollar Condition ($)	Low Dollar Condition ($)	Control Dollar Condition ($)
134	77	100
156	65	85
134	87	89
132	100	94
164	88	88
127	68	103
135	86	88
134	73	93
133	69	78
151	87	82
$\Sigma HD = 1{,}400$	$\Sigma LD = 800$	$\Sigma C = 900$
Mean = 140	Mean = 80	Mean = 90

Recall that Σ, or the symbol for sigma, means "the sum of." Thus Σ_{HD} is the sum of the scores for the High Dollar Condition. That is, $134 + 156 + 134 + 132 + 164 + 127 + 135 + 134 + 133 + 151 = 1{,}400$. There are 10 scores here, so we divide $1{,}400 / 10 = 140$, giving us our mean of 140. We do the same thing for the Low Dollar Condition, with a mean of 80. Finally, we do the same for Σ_C, giving us a mean of 90 ($900 / 10 = 90$).

For the first part of our analysis, we compare the means. As you see, $140 in the High Dollar Condition is much higher than both $80 in the

Low Dollar Condition and $90 in the Control Dollar Condition. If I were "eyeballing" this, I would think that participants recalled spending more in the high condition than both the low and control, though I don't think the low and control differ. However, just because some of our means *seem* to differ doesn't mean they *do* differ. To make that assessment, we run the one-way ANOVA and look at the *p* value to see if it is less than .05. We can do this by hand-or we can take the easy road and let SPSS calculate it for us. I am going to take the easy road, but keep in mind that we still have to interpret what SPSS tells us.

For the next section, I am going to open SPSS and run a one-way ANOVA. I'll use screenshots from SPSS as I go, but you can run these analyses yourself. Just set up your SPSS file like mine (or download the Crash Course in Inferential Statistics—The One-Way ANOVA SPSS file from the website at **study.sagepub.com/winter**). I am just going to give you the basics here, but you can refer to other sources to figure out some of the information we get from the one-way ANOVA not covered in this chapter (like homogeneity of variance, Welch test, etc.).

SPSS: OUR BOOK SURVEY STUDY

1. Click Analyze > Compare Means > One-Way ANOVA . . . on the top menu as shown in the following screenshot.

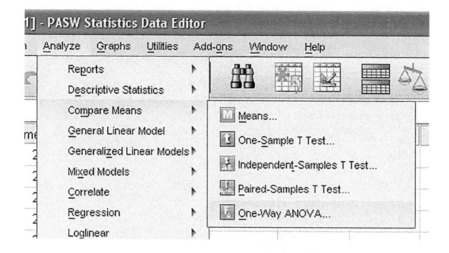

You will be presented with the following:

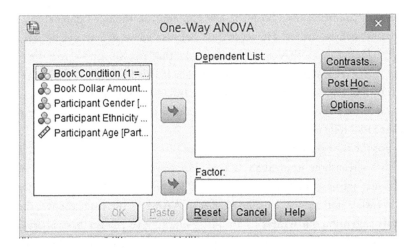

2. Move the independent variable into the Factor box and the dependent variable into the Dependent List box by highlighting the relevant variables and clicking the ⬇ buttons. Note that SPSS uses different names for variables. It calls the dependent variable the Dependent List, and it calls the independent variable the Factor. Just remember that our dependent variable must be scaled in order to run this test (1 to 9, or 1 to 5, or even 0 to 100,000). The independent variable must be categorical, though with a One Way ANOVA we can now look at more than two levels (dressy vs. sloppy vs. casual, old vs. middle-aged vs. young, Republican vs. Democrat v. Independent, high vs. medium vs. low, etc.).

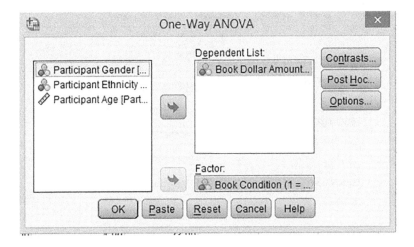

3. Click the Post Hoc button and tick the Tukey checkbox as shown in the following screenshot. There are lots of choices, as you can see, but I tend to use Tukey, which isn't too strict (letting me avoid a Type II error) or too lenient (letting me avoid a Type I error).

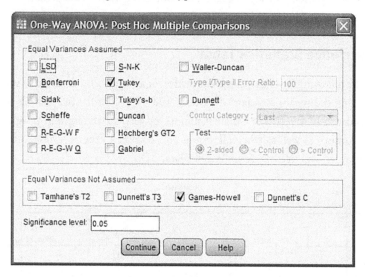

If we find that our ANOVA is significant, we will know only that at least one mean differs from another mean. The post hoc test will tell you which means actually differ.

4. Click the Options button. Tick the Descriptive and Means plot checkboxes in the Statistics area as shown in the following screenshot.

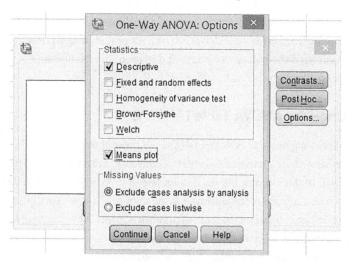

Click the Continue button. Then click the OK button.

OUTPUT OF THE ONE-WAY ANOVA IN SPSS

You will be presented with several tables containing all the data generated by the One-Way ANOVA procedure in SPSS.

Descriptive Statistics Table

The following descriptives table provides some very useful descriptive statistics including the mean, standard deviation, and 95% confidence intervals for the dependent variable (Book Dollar Amount) for each separate group (High, Low, and Control) as well as when all groups are combined (Total). These figures are useful when you need to describe your data.

Descriptives

Book Dollar Amount

	N	Mean	Std. Deviation	Std. Error	95% Confidence Interval for Mean Lower Bound	95% Confidence Interval for Mean Upper Bound	Minimum	Maximum
High	10	140.00	12.329	3.899	131.18	148.82	127	164
Low	10	80.00	11.284	3.568	71.93	88.07	65	100
Control	10	90.00	7.717	2.440	84.48	95.52	78	103
Total	30	103.33	28.597	5.221	92.65	114.01	65	164

As you can see, we have 10 participants in the High Condition, 10 participants in the Low Condition, and 10 participants in the Control Condition. The mean for the High condition is 140 ($SD = 12.33$), the mean for the Low Condition is 80 ($SD = 11.28$), and the mean for the Control Condition is 90 ($SD = 7.72$). We can ignore the standard error, confidence interval, minimum, and maximum for now, but we will need the means and standard deviation information in our write-up, so we'll come back to this table.

The One-Way ANOVA Table (ANOVA)

The following one-way ANOVA table shows the output of the ANOVA analysis and whether we have a statistically significant difference between our group means. We can see that in this example the significance level is .000, well below .05. Therefore, there is a statistically significant difference in the amount of money participants recalled spending on books based on the recall of prior participants. This is great to know, but what is unknown is which of the specific groups differed. Luckily, we can find this out in the multiple comparisons table, which contains the results of post hoc tests.

ANOVA

Book Dollar Amount

	Sum of Squares	df	Mean Square	F	Sig.
Between Groups	20666.667	2	10333.333	91.475	.000
Within Groups	3050.000	27	112.963		
Total	23716.667	29			

Multiple Comparisons Table

From the results so far we know that there are significant differences between the groups as a whole. The following post hoc table, or multiple comparisons table, shows which groups differed from each other. The Tukey post hoc test is generally the preferred test for conducting post hoc tests on a one-way ANOVA, but there are many others. We can see from this table that there is a significant difference in recalled money spent on textbooks between the High and Low Dollar Conditions ($p = .000$) as well as between the High and Control Conditions ($p = .000$). However, there were no differences between the Low and Control Conditions ($p = .108$).

Post Hoc Tests

Multiple Comparisons

Dependent Variable: Book Dollar Amount
Tukey HSD

(I) Book Condition (1 = High, 2 = Low, 3 = Control)	(J) Book Condition (1 = High, 2 = Low, 3 = Control)	Mean Difference (I-J)	Std. Error	Sig.	95% Confidence Interval	
					Lower Bound	Upper Bound
High	Low	60.000*	4.753	.000	48.21	71.79
	Control	50.000*	4.753	.000	38.21	61.79
Low	High	-60.000*	4.753	.000	-71.79	-48.21
	Control	-10.000	4.753	.108	-21.79	1.79
Control	High	-50.000*	4.753	.000	-61.79	-38.21
	Low	10.000	4.753	.108	-1.79	21.79

*. The mean difference is significant at the 0.05 level.

REPORTING THE OUTPUT OF THE ONE-WAY ANOVA

We report the statistics in this format: F(degrees of freedom[df]) = F-value, p = significance level. In our case this is $F(2, 27) = 91.48, p < .001$, and our means/SDs are ($M = 140, SD = 12.33$) for the High Dollar Condition,

(M = **80**, SD = **11.28**) for the Low Dollar Condition, and (M = **90**, SD = **7.72**) for the Control Condition. We would report the results of the study as follows:

> We ran a one-way ANOVA with book condition (high, low, or control) as our independent variable and amount spent on books as our dependent variable. The one-way ANOVA was significant, $F(2, 27) = 91.48, p < .001$. Tukey post hoc tests revealed that students recalled spending more money on books in the High Dollar Condition ($M = 140, SD = 12.33$) than in both the Low Dollar Condition ($M = 80, SD = 11.28$) and the Control Condition ($M = 90, SD = 7.72$). However, participants did not differ in the amount of money they recalled spending between the Low Dollar and Control Conditions.

That's it! Not too hard, right? Note that I provided means and standard deviations for each of our three conditions. Just remember the basics here: We

FIGURE 4.1 ■ Means Plot – Book Survey Condition (IV) and Book Dollar Amount Recalled (DV)

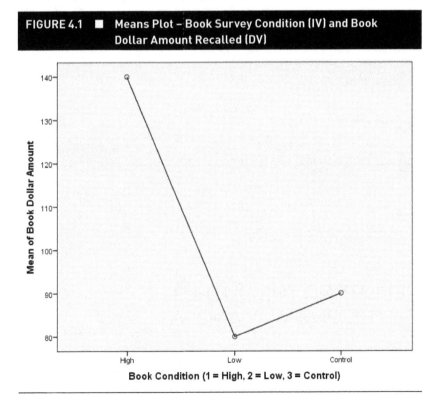

use a one-way ANOVA to look at the differences between three or more means to see if the means differ significantly. We need three SPSS tables to make this assessment: the descriptive statistics tables, the one-way ANOVA table, and the post hoc table.

You will notice in the data file that I included demographic characteristics. Make sure to run descriptives and frequencies on this participant data, which would go in the participant section of a journal-style article. Since I added in 10 new participants for the Control Condition, these descriptive statistics will differ from prior crash courses.

Crash Course in Inferential Statistics (One-Way ANOVA): Quiz Yourself!

Instructions: Imagine you do a study asking only female participants if they are willing to participate in a study. Your experiment has three conditions. In Condition 1, you tell potential participants the study will take 5 minutes. In Condition 2, you tell potential participants the study will take 60 minutes. In Condition 3, you do not tell participants how long the study will take (this is your control group). You then measure their willingness to participate in the study on a scale ranging from 1 (not at all willing) to 9 (very willing). Complete the following questions.

1. What is the independent variable in this study?

    A. Participant's willingness to participate in the study

    B. Participant's ability to participate in the study

    C. The three conditions (60 minutes, 5 minutes, control/no info)

    D. The four conditions (60 minutes, 5 minutes, control/no info, gender)

    E. The gender of the participant (in this case female)

2. What is the dependent variable in this study?

    A. Participant's willingness to participate in the study

    B. Participant's ability to participate in the study

    C. The three conditions (60 minutes, 5 minutes, control/no info)

    D. The four conditions (60 minutes, 5 minutes, control/no info, gender)

    E. The gender of the participant (in this case female)

You run a one-way AVOVA on this data set and get the following SPSS output. Using this output, interpret the information.

(Continued)

(Continued)

Descriptives

Willingness to participate

	N	Mean	Std. Deviation	Std. Error	95% Confidence Interval for Mean		Minimum	Maximum
					Lower Bound	Upper Bound		
5 Minutes	30	7.9333	.73968	.13505	7.6571	8.2095	7.00	9.00
60 Minutes	30	2.0667	.69149	.12625	1.8085	2.3249	1.00	3.00
Control	30	5.7667	1.07265	.19584	5.3661	6.1672	4.00	8.00
Total	90	5.2556	2.57717	.27166	4.7158	5.7953	1.00	9.00

ANOVA

Willingness to participate

	Sum of Squares	df	Mean Square	F	Sig.
Between Groups	528.022	2	264.011	364.009	.000
Within Groups	63.100	87	.725		
Total	591.122	89			

Post Hoc Tests

Multiple Comparisons

Dependent Variable: Willingness to participate
Tukey HSD

(I) IV Time	(J) IV Time	Mean Difference (I-J)	Std. Error	Sig.	95% Confidence Interval	
					Lower Bound	Upper Bound
5 Minutes	60 Minutes	5.86667*	.21989	.000	5.3423	6.3910
	Control	2.16667*	.21989	.000	1.6423	2.6910
60 Minutes	5 Minutes	-5.86667*	.21989	.000	-6.3910	-5.3423
	Control	-3.70000*	.21989	.000	-4.2243	-3.1757
Control	5 Minutes	-2.16667*	.21989	.000	-2.6910	-1.6423
	60 Minutes	3.70000*	.21989	.000	3.1757	4.2243

*. The mean difference is significant at the 0.05 level.

3.   What are the correct means and standard deviations for the 5-Minute, 60-Minute, and Control Conditions?

   A. 5-Minute Condition ($M = 5.87$, $SD = 1.07$); 60-Minute Condition ($M = 7.93$, $SD = 0.73$); Control Condition ($M = 2.07$, $SD = 0.069$)

   B. 5-Minute Condition ($M = 7.93$, $SD = 5.87$); 60-Minute Condition ($M = 2.07$, $SD = 2.17$); Control Condition ($M = 5.76$, $SD = 3.70$)

   C. 5-Minute Condition ($M = 7.93$, $SD = 0.22$); 60-Minute Condition ($M = 2.07$, $SD = 0.22$); Control Condition ($M = 5.76$, $SD = 0.22$)

   D. 5-Minute Condition ($M = 7.93$, $SD = 0.74$); 60-Minute Condition ($M = 2.07$, $SD = 0.69$); Control Condition ($M = 5.77$, $SD = 1.07$)

   E. 5-Minute Condition ($M = 5.87$, $SD = 0.73$); 60-Minute Condition ($M = 7.93$, $SD = 0.069$); Control Condition ($M = 2.07$, $SD = 1.07$)

4.   Is the one-way ANOVA significant? If so, what is the correct APA format for the write-up?

   A. It is not significant.

   B. It is significant, $F(2, 89) = 264.01$, $p < .001$.

C. It is significant, $F(1, 87) = 364.01, p < .001$.

D. It is significant, $F(2, 89) = 364.01, p < .001$.

E. It is significant, $F(2, 87) = 364.01, p < .001$.

5. Finally, which of the following would you use to write up the results in an APA-formatted results section?

A. We ran a one-way ANOVA with the time condition as our independent variable and willingness as our dependent variable. The one-way ANOVA was not significant, $F(2, 87) = 364.01, p > .05$. Thus participants were equally willing to do the study in the 5-Minute Condition ($M = 7.93, SD = 0.73$), the 60-Minute Condition ($M = 2.07, SD = 0.07$), and the Control Condition ($M = 5.76, SD = 1.07$).

B. We ran a one-way ANOVA with the time condition as our independent variable and willingness as our dependent variable. The one-way ANOVA was significant, $F(1, 87) = 364.01, p < .001$. Tukey post hoc tests revealed that participants were more willing to do the study in the 5-Minute Condition ($M = 7.93, SD = 0.73$) than either the 60-Minute Condition ($M = 2.07, SD = 0.07$) or Control Condition ($M = 5.76, SD = 1.07$). In addition, those in the Control Condition were more willing to participate than those in the 60-Minute Condition.

C. We ran a one-way ANOVA with the time condition as our independent variable and willingness as our dependent variable. The one-way ANOVA was significant, $F(2, 89) = 364.01, p < .001$. Tukey post hoc tests revealed that participants were more willing to do the study in the 5-Minute Condition ($M = 7.93, SD = 0.73$) than either the 60-Minute Condition ($M = 2.07, SD = 0.07$) or Control Condition ($M = 5.76, SD = 1.07$). In addition, those in the Control Condition were more willing to participate than those in the 60-Minute Condition.

D. We ran a one-way ANOVA with the time condition as our independent variable and willingness as our dependent variable. The one-way ANOVA was significant, $F(2, 87) = 364.01, p < .001$. Tukey post hoc tests revealed that participants were more willing to do the study in the 5-Minute Condition ($M = 7.93, SD = 0.73$) than either the 60-Minute Condition ($M = 2.07, SD = 0.07$) or Control Condition ($M = 5.76, SD = 1.07$). However, those in the Control Condition did not differ in their willingness to participate from those in the 60-Minute Condition.

E. We ran a one-way ANOVA with the time condition as our independent variable and willingness as our dependent variable. The one-way ANOVA was significant, $F(2, 87) = 364.01, p < .001$. Tukey post hoc tests revealed that participants were more willing to do the study in the 5-Minute Condition ($M = 7.93, SD = 0.74$) than either the 60-Minute Condition ($M = 2.07, SD = 0.69$) or Control Condition ($M = 5.77, SD = 1.07$). In addition, those in the Control Condition were more willing to participate than those in the 60-Minute Condition.

5

THE FACTORIAL
(OR TWO-WAY) ANOVA

What follows is a quick reminder of inferential statistics (focusing on the factorial ANOVA). Quiz yourself on the factorial ANOVA at the end of this chapter!

HOW, WHEN, AND WHY
DO A TWO-WAY ANOVA?

A factorial ANOVA is very similar to both the *t*-test and the one-way ANOVA, but here we compare four or more conditions from two or more independent variables to see if they differ significantly from one another. The easiest factorial design is a 2 × 2 ANOVA (two IVs with two levels each), though it can get more complex depending on the needs of the researcher (a 2 × 3 study, a 2 × 4 study, a 3 × 3 study, etc.). We could get even more complex with more than two IVs (like a 2 × 2 × 2 study or a 2 × 3 × 4 × 5 study!), but in this chapter we will stick with a simple 2 × 2 design (two IVs, two levels each). In this analysis, we need three pieces of information: (1) the means for each of the four conditions (descriptive statistics), (2) the two-way ANOVA information itself, and (3) simple effects tests for any significant interactions (this is a lot like a post hoc tests, but for factorial designs).

1. Once again, remember that a *mean* is the average score for that condition. That is, you add up all of the scores in a condition and divide by the number of total scores to arrive at the average. Since a factorial ANOVA looks at four conditions, we have at least four means: one

for each condition. The means here (plus the standard deviation) are *descriptive statistics*. That is, they help *describe* the data.

2. The factorial ANOVA information itself is a test of *inferential statistics*. That is, we *infer* significant differences between the four groups. But rather than just one F test for the factorial ANOVA, we have three different F tests: one for the main effect of Variable A, one for the main effect of Variable B, and one for the interaction of A × B. When writing it out, you will see a very common layout for the factorial ANOVA, but there will be three F tests. That is, there will be a main effect for Variable A: $F(2, 134) = 2.61, p = .021$. There will be a main effect for Variable B: $F(2, 134) = 3.55, p = .022$. And there will be an interaction for A × B: $F(2, 134) = 1.23, p > .05$. The F tells you that each analysis is an ANOVA. The 2 and 134 tell us our degrees of freedom for each F test. The 2.61 is the actual number for the Variable A main effect, the 3.55 is for the Variable B main effect, and the 1.23 is for the interaction of A × B. The p indicates whether each ANOVA is significant (if it is less than .05, then it is significant).

3. Finally, we have to consider simple effects tests. These are essentially the post hoc tests for a significant interaction. Before getting to that, consider the main effects. Here, we look only at one of our variables independent of the other. For example, Variable A might be our book survey variable. If we have a significant main effect for Variable A, we know we have a difference among the levels for this first variable. That is, students may recall spending different amounts for their book depending on whether they saw prior students report high or low amounts. As with the *t*-test, we go back and look at the means. If students recall spending $140 on books in the High Dollar Condition and $80 in the Low Dollar Condition, then we can easily say, "Participants recall spending more money on books when prior participants recalled spending high dollar amounts than when prior participants recalled spending low dollar amounts." The same thing occurs for Variable B. Let's say we look at males versus females as our second independent variable. We look at the means when the main effect is significant ("Males recall spending more on books than females"). Since the main effect looks at only two means in this example, all we have to do when it is significant is see which of the two means is higher. Easy, right? The tough part comes when we have a significant interaction of A and B. Here we are dealing with four means (the mean for High Dollar Condition males, the mean for High

Dollar Condition females, the mean for Low Dollar Condition males, and the mean for Low Dollar Condition females). If our interaction is significant, we can't tell just by looking at the means which of the four means differ. High Dollar Condition males may differ from High Dollar Condition females but not Low Dollar Condition males or Low Dollar Condition females. Or maybe Low Dollar Condition males recall spending less than High Dollar Condition males, who recall spending more than Low Dollar Condition females but at the same rate as High Dollar Condition females. With four means to compare, we can't simply look to see which mean is higher because it may *look* higher but may not really be *significantly* higher. Thus we need to run a simple effects test on the significant interaction. There are a few ways to do this.

First, you can ignore females altogether. Looking at males only, run a *t*-test to see if the High and Low Dollar Conditions differ. Then, ignore males and run a *t*-test to see if High Dollar Condition females differ from Low Dollar Condition females. Then, ignore the Low Dollar Condition and run a *t*-test to see if High Dollar Condition males differ from High Dollar Condition females. Finally, ignore the High Dollar Condition and run a *t*-test see if Low Dollar Condition males differ from Low Dollar Condition females. Thus four *t*-tests get at all of the comparisons possible for the means.

Second, you can do the same thing but this time run a one-way ANOVA for each two condition comparison (one-way ANOVA for High Dollar Condition males vs. High Dollar Condition females, one-way ANOVA for Low Dollar Condition males vs. Low Dollar Condition females, one-way ANOVA for High Dollar Condition males vs. Low Dollar Condition males, and one-way ANOVA for High Dollar Condition females vs. Low Dollar Condition females). I actually prefer this method, as it keeps you within the ANOVA analysis. It also helps if one of your independent variables has more than two levels (like a 2 × 3 design) so that you can run a Tukey post hoc test on that independent variable with three level variables when you run simple-effect tests.

There are other ways of running simple effects tests, but the second one above is my recommendation. In the end, for each dependent variable that you look at, there will be up to seven different F tests: (1) main effect Variable A, (2) main effect Variable B, (3) interaction A × B, (4) simple effect Variable A within level one of Variable B, (5) simple effect of Variable A within level two of Variable B, (6) simple effect of Variable B within level one of Variable A, (7) simple effect of Variable B within level two of Variable A. Before looking at the SPSS data, just a few reminders:

As with the *t*-test and one-way ANOVA, we run a factorial ANOVA only under certain conditions.

> First, our dependent variable (the variable we measure) must be continuous/ scaled. That is, the DV has to be along a scale. For example, it can be an attitude ("On a scale of 1 to 9, how angry are you?") or a time frame ("How quickly did the salesperson help the customer on a scale of zero seconds to a thousand seconds?"). We call these interval or ratio scales. We *cannot* run a factorial ANOVA on categorical data. That is, if we have a yes/no question ("Are you lonely: yes or no") or a category-based question ("What is your favorite food: hamburgers, pizza, salad, or tacos?"), then we cannot run a factorial ANOVA. These latter questions are based more on choice of option rather than an actual rating scale, and thus we cannot use a factorial ANOVA on them.

> Second, we run a factorial ANOVA when we have two independent variables in the same design. (Note: There must be at least two levels for each IV.) For the analysis, we will always report the main effect for Variable A, the main effect for Variable B, and the interaction for A × B. If the interaction is not significant, we can stop. However, if the interaction is significant, then we need to include follow-up simple effects tests.

Let's see how this looks using our book survey example.

An Example: Social Influence and College Textbooks

Let's use the study we began in the chapter on descriptive statistics. A robust finding in social psychology is that when people have insufficient information about how to behave or what decision to make, they rely on others as a source of information. Imagine we ask college student participants how much money they spent on books last semester. We have them fill out their name and the amount of money they recall spending at the bottom of a book survey after the names and amounts listed by 10 prior participants. Unknown to our participants, we alter the amounts recalled by the 10 prior participants, creating one condition with a high average book price ($150) and one condition with a low average book price ($75). But here we add in a second independent variable, looking at the gender of the participant (male vs. female). We predict a main effect of book condition (those in the high condition will recall spending more on books than those in the low condition). We predict a main effect of gender (females will recall spending less than males—note that I am just making this up!). We also predict an interaction (females, but not males, will recall spending more money in the high condition than in the low condition—again, making this up!). We collect signatures and dollar amounts from 20 real participants randomly assigned to the High Dollar Condition and 20 real participants randomly assigned to the Low Dollar Condition. In each condition, there are 10 males and 10 females. Their data are as follows.

	High Dollar Condition	Low Dollar Condition	
Women	145	84	
	130	100	
	125	94	
	165	92	
	135	88	
	143	83	
	143	87	
	139	90	
	150	87	
	125	95	
	M = 140	*M* = 90	All Women *M* = 115
Men	115	100	
	123	87	
	98	105	
	103	108	
	110	95	
	115	98	
	101	95	
	126	102	
	109	110	
	100	100	
	M = 110	*M* = 100	All Men *M* = 105
	All High *M* = 125	All Low *M* = 95	

For the first part of our analysis, we compare the means. But which ones? Note that there are eight different means here! So let's start with the *gender main effect*. Eyeballing it, females seem to recall spending more ($M = 115$) than males ($M = 105$). I'm not sure if that is statistically different, though. Let's also look at the *dollar amount main effect*. Eyeballing this, participants seem to recall spending more in the High Dollar Condition ($M = 125$) than the Low Dollar Condition ($M = 95$). I'm sure this one will be significant. But we also need to consider the interactions. Eyeballing this, I would say that female participants in the High Dollar Condition ($M = 140$) recall spending more than all other conditions (high condition males $M = 110$, low condition males $M = 100$, and low condition females $M = 90$). But we'll have to see if that is a significant difference using our factorial ANOVA.

For the next section, I am going to open SPSS and run a factorial (or univariate) ANOVA. I'll use screenshots from SPSS as I go, but you can also run these analyses yourself. Just set up your SPSS file like mine (or download the Crash Course in Inferential Statistics—The Factorial ANOVA SPSS file from the website at **study .sagepub.com/winter**). I am just going to give you the basics here, but you can refer to other sources to figure out some of the information we get from the factorial ANOVA not covered in this lecture (like homogeneity of variance, Welch test, etc.).

SPSS: OUR BOOK SURVEY STUDY

1. Click Analyze > General Linear Model > Univariate . . . on the top menu as shown in the following screenshot. (Note: A general linear model usually implies some kind of factorial design.)

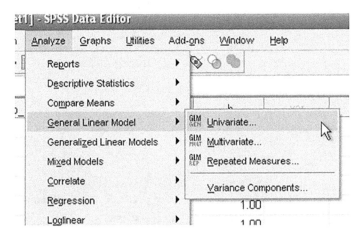

You will be presented with the following:

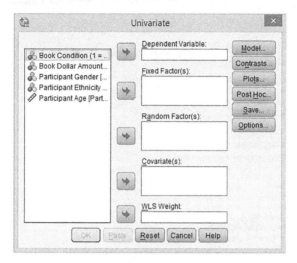

2. Put both the **Book Condition (1 = High, 2 = Low)** and **Gender (Men = 1, Women = 2)** variables into the Fixed Factor(s) box. (Note: I could easily have assigned Men = 2 and Women = 1. The assignment of a number here is arbitrary, as this is a nominal variable.) Move the **Book Dollar Amount** variable into the Dependent Variable box by highlighting the relevant variables and clicking the ![button] buttons. Just remember that our dependent variable must be scaled in order to run this test (1 to 9, or 1 to 5, or even 0 to 100,000). The independent variable must be categorical (sloppy vs. casual, old vs. young, Republican vs. Democrat, high vs. low, etc.).

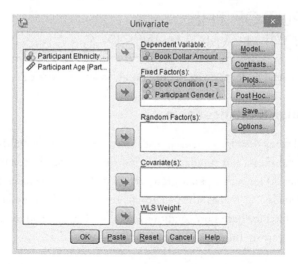

Click the [Options...] button. Tick the Descriptive statistics box as shown in the following screenshot and then click the [Continue] button. Then click the [OK] button.

OUTPUT OF THE FACTORIAL ANOVA IN SPSS

There are several tables to cover in our output, so let's get started!

Descriptive Statistics Table

The following descriptives table provides some very useful descriptive statistics, including the mean and standard deviation for the dependent variable (Book Dollar Amount) for each separate group (High males, High females, Low males, and Low females), as well as when all groups are combined (Total for both High conditions, total for both Low conditions, total for females, and total for males). These figures are useful when you need to *describe* your data.

Descriptive Statistics

Dependent Variable: Book Dollar Amount

Book Condition (1 = High, 2 = Low)	Participant Gender (1 = Men, 2 = Women)	Mean	Std. Deviation	N
High	Males	110.00	9.718	10
	Females	140.00	12.220	10
	Total	125.00	18.770	20
Low	Males	100.00	6.799	10
	Females	90.00	5.292	10
	Total	95.00	7.841	20
Total	Males	105.00	9.641	20
	Females	115.00	27.238	20
	Total	110.00	20.793	40

As you can see, we have 10 females in the high condition, 10 males in the high condition, 10 females in the low condition, and 10 males in the low condition. We will need the means and *SD* information in our write-up, so we'll come back to this table. Keep in mind that high condition (total) has a mean of **125**, **SD** = **18.77** while the low condition (total) has a mean of **95**, **SD** = **7.84**. Males (total) have a mean of **105**, **SD** = **9.64** while females (total) have a mean of **115**, **SD** = **27.24**. Getting more specific, high condition males have a mean of **110**, **SD** = **9.72**, while low condition males have a mean of **100**, **SD** = **6.80**. Finally, high condition females have a mean of **140**, **SD** = **12.22**, while low condition females have a mean of **90**, **SD** = **5.29**. So a lot of means here! (Eight of which are important; the Total/Total with *N* = 40 at the bottom is the only one we won't pay attention to in our write-up.)

The Factorial ANOVA Table
(Tests of Between Subjects Effects)

The factorial ANOVA table (which SPSS calls the Tests of Between-Subjects Effects) shows the output of the ANOVA analysis and whether we have a statistically significant difference between our group means for both of our main effects and our interaction. Let's focus on the rows that are most helpful for us.

First, find the IVBook$Condition row. This is our main effect for the book amount independent variable. The *F* value is 113.21, with *p* = .000. Thus we have a significant book survey condition main effect. We focus on our degrees of freedom for IVBook$Condition (1, 36). The 1 comes from the *df* for the IVBook$Condition row, while the 36 comes from the Error row. I'll show you how to write this up in a moment, but now look at the main effect for ParticipantGender. This is also significant. The F value is 12.58, $p = .001$. The df, again, is (1, 36). Finally, look at the interaction of IVBook\$Condition × ParticipantGender, which is significant $F(1, 36) = 50.31, p < .001$.

Tests of Between-Subjects Effects

Dependent Variable: Book Dollar Amount

Source	Type III Sum of Squares	df	Mean Square	F	Sig.
Corrected Model	14000.000[a]	3	4666.667	58.700	.000
Intercept	484000.000	1	484000.000	6088.050	.000
IVBook$Condition	9000.000	1	9000.000	113.208	.000
ParticipantGender	1000.000	1	1000.000	12.579	.001
IVBook$Condition * ParticipantGender	4000.000	1	4000.000	50.314	.000
Error	2862.000	36	79.500		
Total	500862.000	40			
Corrected Total	16862.000	39			

a. R Squared = .830 (Adjusted R Squared = .816)

REPORTING THE OUTPUT OF THE TWO-WAY ANOVA (PART I: WITH A NONSIGNIFICANT INTERACTION)

As you see in this heading, this is only Part I of our reporting. Right now, we can report the main effects and the first part of the interaction, but we will need to do some additional simple effects tests for a significant interaction. Before doing simple effects tests, I want to focus on our main effects. Similar to the one-way ANOVA, we report the statistics in this format: F(degrees of freedom[df]) = F-value, p = significance level for each main effect.

1. For the main effect of IVBook\$Condition, this would be: $F(1, 36) = $ **113.21, $p < .001$,** and our means/SDs would be ($M = 125$, $SD = 18.77$) for the High Dollar Condition and ($M = 95$, $SD = 7.84$) for the Low Dollar Condition (remember to look back at the descriptives table to find these means and standard deviations).

2. Next, we look at the ParticipantGender row. We have a main effect here, $F(1, 36) = 12.58, p = .001$, with female participants ($M = 115$, $SD = 27.24$)

recalling spending more money on books than male participants (*M* = **105,** *SD* = **9.64**).

We would report the results of the study for these main effects as follows:

We ran a factorial ANOVA with book survey condition and gender as our independent variables and amount participants recalled spending on books as our dependent variable. There was a significant main effect for book survey condition, *F*(**1, 36**) = **113.21**, *p* < **.001**, with participants recalling spending more money on books in the high condition (*M* = **125**, *SD* = **18.77**) than in the low condition (*M* = **95**, *SD* = **7.84**). Similarly, there was a significant main effect for gender, *F*(**1, 36**) = **12.58**, *p* = **.001**. with female participants (*M* = **115**, *SD* = **27.24**) recalling spending more money on books than male participants (*M* = **105**, *SD* = **9.64**).

Now, look at the IVBook$Condition*ParticipantGender row. As you can see, the interaction between our two independent variables is significant (*p* < .001). Because this interaction is significant, the main effects are qualified by a significant interaction. We need to run simple effects tests on the interaction. I will discuss simple effects in the next section (Part II), but for now I want to *pretend* that the interaction was not significant. *If* this is the case, we would conclude our statistics paragraph with the following:

There was no significant interaction of book survey condition and gender, *F*(**1, 36**) = **????**, *p* > **.05**. There was no difference in spending recall between high condition males (*M* = 110, *SD* = 9.72), low condition males (*M* = 100, *SD* = 6.80), high condition females (*M* = 140, *SD* = 12.22), and low condition females (*M* = 90, *SD* = 7.84).

If our interaction was not significant, we are done. Unfortunately (or fortunately, depending on your need to support your hypothesis!), we have a significant interaction to look at because it actually is significant. We will use our significant *F* interaction in our actual final write-up: *F*(1, 36) = 50.31, *p* < .001. That is, we would write:

The main effects were qualified by a significant interaction of participant gender and book survey condition, *F*(1, 36) = 50.31, *p* < .001.

Now it is time to tease apart the interaction so we can compare the four conditions. This is where our simple effects analysis will come into play.

SPSS: OUR BOOK SURVEY STUDY (PART II: SIGNIFICANT INTERACTION— SIMPLE EFFECTS TESTING)

After running our factorial ANOVA, we look at the data to see if the interaction was significant or nonsignificant. We just saw what to do with a nonsignificant interaction, but now we must figure out what to do with a significant interaction. There are several ways of doing follow-up simple effects tests, including running t-tests or one-way ANOVAs that hold one IV constant while looking at differences among the two levels of the remaining IV. We could also use *syntax* in SPSS, but this is a little more complicated than I want to cover here. I'm only going to show you the easiest way of getting at simple effects. It involves holding one IV constant and looking at differences between the levels of the second IV. We will use the ANOVA for this rather than a t-test, since I really want you to focus on the General Linear Model for 2×2 factorial designs.

Basically, we are going to look at differences between two levels of one of our IVs while holding the other IV constant. For example, let's hold gender constant. (1) We will first look only at males. We will see if book survey recall differs between high condition males and low condition males. (2) Then we will look only at females. We will see if book survey recall differs between high condition females and low condition females. (3) Next, we hold book survey condition constant. Looking only at the high condition, we will see if book survey recall for high condition males differs from book survey recall for high condition females. (4) Finally, we look only at the low condition, trying to see if book survey recall differs between low condition males and low condition females. Note that we are looking at four simple effects tests here. Make sense? Here's how we do it!

1. Select Data > Split File.

2. Select your independent variable (Book Condition). Click OK.

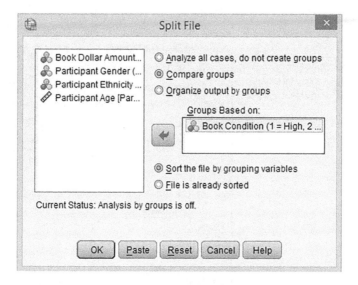

3. Now, rerun your original General Linear Model, but this time remove Book Condition from your Fixed Factor(s) box. That is, since we used our split file and selected Book Condition, we no longer use Book Condition as a fixed factor in this ANOVA. You will see in the results that we now have output for the high condition alone (where we can look at males vs. females) as well as output for the low condition alone (where we can look at males vs. females). Make sure to go into the Options box and select descriptive statistics.

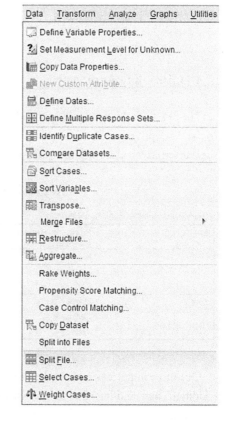

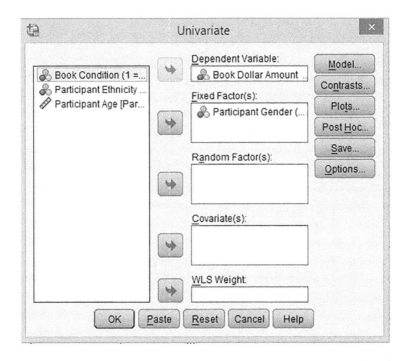

4. Click OK to get the output.

The first few tables you will see involve descriptive statistics. These are similar to the descriptives we saw from our original factorial ANOVA. Pay attention to these descriptives, as we will refer back to them for the means in our write-up.

Descriptive Statistics

Dependent Variable: Book Dollar Amount

Book Condition (1 = High, 2 = Low)	Participant Gender (1 = Men, 2 = Women)	Mean	Std. Deviation	N
High	Males	110.00	9.718	10
	Females	140.00	12.220	10
	Total	125.00	18.770	20
Low	Males	100.00	6.799	10
	Females	90.00	5.292	10
	Total	95.00	7.841	20

Our most important table is the next one, which looks at each book survey condition (high and low) and tells us whether there is an effect for gender within each level.

Tests of Between-Subjects Effects

Dependent Variable: Book Dollar Amount

Book Condition (1 = High, 2 = Low)	Source	Type III Sum of Squares	df	Mean Square	F	Sig.
High	Corrected Model	4500.000[a]	1	4500.000	36.919	.000
	Intercept	312500.000	1	312500.000	2563.810	.000
	ParticipantGender	4500.000	1	4500.000	36.919	.000
	Error	2194.000	18	121.889		
	Total	319194.000	20			
	Corrected Total	6694.000	19			
Low	Corrected Model	500.000[b]	1	500.000	13.473	.002
	Intercept	180500.000	1	180500.000	4863.772	.000
	ParticipantGender	500.000	1	500.000	13.473	.002
	Error	668.000	18	37.111		
	Total	181668.000	20			
	Corrected Total	1168.000	19			

a. R Squared = .672 (Adjusted R Squared = .654)

b. R Squared = .428 (Adjusted R Squared = .396)

Look only at the high condition numbers, and focus on the ParticipantGender row. You'll see that it is significant, $F(1, 18) = 36.92$, $p < .001$. That is, there is a significant difference between high condition males (**M = 110, SD = 9.72**) and high condition females (**M = 140, SD = 12.22**), with females recalling spending more on books. There was also a significant difference between males and females in the low condition, $F(1, 18) = 13.47$, $p = .002$, with low condition males (**M = 100, SD = 6.80**) recalling spending more than low condition females (**M = 90, SD = 5.29**). Your official write-up would look like this:

> First, simple effects tests show a difference between males and females in the High Dollar Condition, $F(1, 18) = 36.92$, $p < .001$. That is, there is a significant difference between high condition males ($M = 110, SD = 9.72$) and high condition females ($M = 140, SD = 12.22$), with females recalling spending more on books. Second, there was also a significant difference between men and women in the Low Dollar Condition, $F(1, 18) = 13.47$, $p = .002$, with low condition males ($M = 100, SD = 6.80$) recalling spending more than low condition females ($M = 90, SD = 5.29$).

We are almost finished. Our next step is to go back and rerun the split files procedure, but this time we will select gender rather than book condition. Then we will rerun the General Linear Model (Univariate ANOVA) to look at differences for different book conditions. Let's do that now.

1. Select Data > Split File.

2. Select your independent variable (Gender). Click OK.

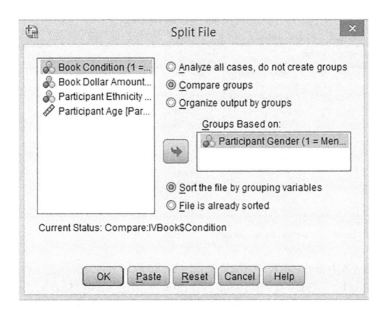

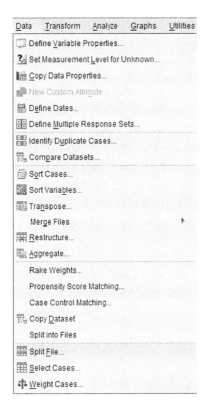

3. Now, rerun your original General Linear Model, but this time remove ParticipantGender from your Fixed Factor(s) box and move IVBook$Condition into that box. That is, since we used our split file and selected ParticipantGender, we no longer need ParticipantGender as an independent variable. You will see in the results that we now have output for males alone (where we can look at the high vs. low conditions) as well as output for females alone (where we can look at the high vs. low conditions). Make sure to go back into the Options box and select descriptive statistics!

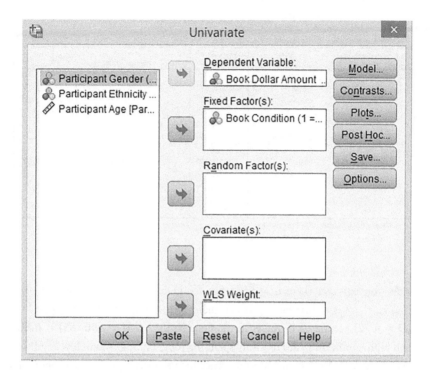

4. Click OK to get the output.

Here, we will get similar tables as in our prior analysis. The descriptives will be identical to those in our prior analysis.

Descriptive Statistics

Dependent Variable: Book Dollar Amount

Participant Gender (1 = Men, 2 = Women)	Book Condition (1 = High, 2 = Low)	Mean	Std. Deviation	N
Males	High	110.00	9.718	10
	Low	100.00	6.799	10
	Total	105.00	9.641	20
Females	High	140.00	12.220	10
	Low	90.00	5.292	10
	Total	115.00	27.238	20

The tests of between-subjects effects, though, will differ now that we split the file differently (based on gender this time rather than book condition).

Tests of Between-Subjects Effects

Dependent Variable: Book Dollar Amount

Participant Gender (1 = Men, 2 = Women)	Source	Type III Sum of Squares	df	Mean Square	F	Sig.
Males	Corrected Model	500.000[a]	1	500.000	7.109	.016
	Intercept	220500.000	1	220500.000	3135.071	.000
	IVBook$Condition	500.000	1	500.000	7.109	.016
	Error	1266.000	18	70.333		
	Total	222266.000	20			
	Corrected Total	1766.000	19			
Females	Corrected Model	12500.000[b]	1	12500.000	140.977	.000
	Intercept	264500.000	1	264500.000	2983.083	.000
	IVBook$Condition	12500.000	1	12500.000	140.977	.000
	Error	1596.000	18	88.667		
	Total	278596.000	20			
	Corrected Total	14096.000	19			

a. R Squared = .283 (Adjusted R Squared = .243)

b. R Squared = .887 (Adjusted R Squared = .880)

As you can see, there is a difference for males, $F(1, 18) = 7.11$, $p = .016$. That is, there is a difference between males in the high condition (**M = 110, SD = 9.72**) compared to males in the low condition (**M = 100, SD = 6.80**), with high condition males recalling spending more on books than low condition males. There is also a significant difference between the high and low conditions for females, $F(1, 18) = 140.98$, $p < .001$. That is, there is a difference between females in the high condition (**M = 140, SD = 12.22**) compared to females in the low condition (**M = 90, SD = 5.29**), with high condition females recalling spending more than low condition females. Your write-up for these last two simple effects test would look like the following:

> Third, simple effects found differences in the High versus Low Dollar Conditions for males, $F(1, 18) = 7.11$, $p = .016$. That is, there is a difference between males in the high condition ($M = 110$, $SD = 9.72$) compared to males in the low condition ($M = 100$, $SD = 6.80$), with high condition males recalling spending more on books than low condition males. Finally, there is also a significant difference between the High and Low Dollar Conditions for females, $F(1, 18) = 140.98$, $p < .001$. That is, there is a difference between females in the high condition ($M = 140$, $SD = 12.22$) compared to females in the low condition ($M = 90$, $SD = 5.29$), with high condition females recalling spending more than low condition females.

Now we are done! We just need to write it up.

REPORTING THE OUTPUT OF THE TWO-WAY ANOVA (PART II: WITH A SIGNIFICANT INTERACTION)

First, repeat our text for the main effects. Second, include the interaction F test as well as all simple effects tests.

> We ran a factorial ANOVA with book survey condition and gender as our independent variables and amount participants recalled spending on books as our dependent variable. There was a significant main effect for book survey condition, $F(1, 36) = 113.21$, $p < .001$, with participants recalling spending more money on books in the high condition ($M = 125$, $SD = 18.77$) than in the low condition ($M = 95$, $SD = 7.84$). Similarly, there was a significant main effect for gender, $F(1, 36) = 12.58$, $p = .001$, with female participants ($M = 115$, $SD = 27.24$) recalling spending more money on books than male participants ($M = 105$, $SD = 9.64$). These main effects were qualified by a significant interaction of gender and book survey condition, $F(1, 36) = 50.31$, $p < .001$. First, simple effects tests show a difference between males and females in the High Dollar Condition, $F(1, 18) = 36.92$, $p < .001$. That is, there is a significant difference between high condition males ($M = 110$, $SD = 9.72$) and high condition females ($M = 140$, $SD = 12.22$), with females recalling spending more on books. Second, there was also a significant difference between men and women in the Low Dollar Condition, $F(1, 18) = 13.47$, $p = .002$, with low condition males ($M = 100$, $SD = 6.80$) recalling spending more than low condition females ($M = 90$, $SD = 5.29$). Third, simple effects found differences in the High versus Low Dollar Conditions for males, $F(1, 18) = 7.11$, $p = .016$. That is, there is a difference between males in the high condition ($M = 110$, $SD = 9.72$) compared to males in the low condition ($M = 100$, $SD = 6.80$), with high condition males recalling spending more on books than low condition males. Finally, there is also a significant difference between the High and Low Dollar Conditions for females, $F(1, 18) = 140.98$, $p < .001$. That is, there is a difference between females in the high condition ($M = 140$, $SD = 12.22$) compared to females in the low condition ($M = 90$, $SD = 5.29$), with high condition females recalling spending more than low condition females.

Now we're done! Of course, given the complicated paragraph format above, we could put our means in a table. It might make the paragraph easier to read. Consider this alternative paragraph and accompanying table.

We ran a factorial ANOVA with book survey condition and gender as our independent variables and amount participants recalled spending on books as our dependent variable. There was a significant main effect for book survey condition, $F(1, 36) = 113.21$, $p < .001$, with participants recalling spending more money on books in the high condition than in the low condition. Similarly, there was a significant main effect for gender, $F(1, 36) = 12.58$, $p = .001$, with female participants recalling spending more money on books than male participants. These main effects were qualified by a significant interaction of gender and book survey condition, $F(1, 36) = 50.31$, $p < .001$. First, simple effects tests show a difference between males and females in the High Dollar Condition, $F(1, 18) = 36.92$, $p < .001$. That is, there is a significant difference between high condition males and high condition females, with females recalling spending more on books. Second, there was also a significant difference between men and women in the Low Dollar Condition, $F(1, 18) = 13.47$, $p = .002$, with low condition males recalling spending more than low condition females. Third, simple effects found differences in the High versus Low Dollar Conditions for males, $F(1, 18) = 7.11$, $p = .016$. That is, there is a difference between males in the high condition compared to males in the low condition, with high condition males recalling spending more on books than low condition males. Finally, there is also a significant difference between the High and Low Dollar Conditions for females, $F(1, 18) = 140.98$, $p < .001$. That is, there is a difference between females in the high condition compared to females in the low condition, with high condition females recalling spending more than low condition females. (See the following table for means and standard deviations.)

	High Dollar Condition	Low Dollar Condition	Total Gender
Women	$M = 140$ $(SD = 12.22)$	$M = 90$ $(SD = 5.29)$	$M = 115$ $(SD = 27.24)$
Men	$M = 110$ $(SD = 9.72)$	$M = 100$ $(SD = 6.80)$	$M = 105$ $(SD = 9.64)$
Total Dollar	$M = 125$ $(SD = 18.77)$	$M = 95$ $(SD = 7.84)$	

Remember to run frequencies and descriptive statistics for the demographic variables in this new data set. It has changed now that we have added more participants to this data set!

Crash Course in Inferential Statistics (Factorial ANOVA): Quiz Yourself!

Instructions: Imagine you want to see how participants interpret their own emotions based on the presence of a drug and another person. You give an injection of epinephrine to all participants, which is a drug that increases general physiological arousal (sweating, heart rate, blood pressure, agitation, etc.). For some participants, you tell them that the drug is inert: It does not have any physiological effects and is basically a placebo. For other participants, you tell them the side effects of the drug include increased physiological arousal, so they think it is real (thus *all* participants feel the arousal of the drug, but only half of them think the drug is causing that arousal). You then put each participant in a room with another "participant" (actually, this person is a confederate in the study!) who acts either really happy or really angry. Later, you test the real participant to assess his or her personal rating of happiness (1 = not at all happy, 9 = extremely happy). You predict that those who are given the drug and think it is a placebo will rate themselves as very happy when they are in the presence of the happy confederate but very angry when in the presence of the angry confederate. However, those who know the drug is real and know it is causing their arousal will not differ in their happiness ratings regardless of whether they see a happy or angry confederate.

Note: DrugThoughts = The participant thinks the drug is either a placebo or real

ConfederateHappyAngry = Confederate acts either happy or angry

1. What are the independent and dependent variables in this study? Choose the best option from this list:

    A. There is one independent variable: the drug manipulation (the participant either thinks the drug is real or thinks it is placebo). There are two dependent variables. First, the behavior of the confederate varies (the confederate is either happy or angry). Second, there is the personal rating of happiness (the participant is either very happy or not happy).

    B. There are three independent variables. First, there is a drug manipulation (the participant either thinks the drug is real or thinks it is placebo). Second, the behavior of the confederate varies (the confederate is either happy or angry). Third, there is the personal rating of happiness (the participant is either very happy or not happy). The dependent variable is whether the participant knows there is a confederate in the study.

    C. There are two independent variables. First, there is a drug manipulation (the participant either thinks the drug is real or thinks it is placebo). Second, there is the personal rating of happiness (the participant is either very happy or not happy). There is one dependent variable: the behavior of the confederate (the confederate is either happy or angry).

    D. There are two independent variables. First, there is a drug manipulation (the participant either thinks the drug is real or thinks it is placebo). Second,

(Continued)

(Continued)

the behavior of the confederate varies (the confederate is either happy or angry). There is one dependent variable: personal rating of happiness.

E. There are two independent variables. First, there is a drug manipulation (the participant either thinks the drug is real or thinks it is placebo). Second, the behavior of the confederate varies (the confederate is either happy or angry). There are two dependent variables as well. First, there is the personal rating of happiness. Second, there are ratings of whether the participants know there is a confederate in the study.

You run a two-way ANOVA on this data set and get the following SPSS output. Using this output, interpret the information.

⇒ **Univariate Analysis of Variance**

[DataSet0]

Between-Subjects Factors

		Value Label	N
Drug (Placebo or Effective)	1.00	Thinks Drug is a Placebo	40
	2.00	Thinks Drug is Real	40
Confederate (Happy or Angry)	1.00	Happy	40
	2.00	Angry	40

Descriptive Statistics

Dependent Variable: Participant Happiness Rating

Drug (Placebo or Effective)	Confederate (Happy or Angry)	Mean	Std. Deviation	N
Thinks Drug is a Placebo	Happy	6.4000	1.14248	20
	Angry	4.2000	1.00525	20
	Total	5.3000	1.53923	40
Thinks Drug is Real	Happy	5.0000	.45883	20
	Angry	4.9500	.51042	20
	Total	4.9750	.47972	40
Total	Happy	5.7000	1.11401	40
	Angry	4.5750	.87376	40
	Total	5.1375	1.14454	80

Tests of Between-Subjects Effects

Dependent Variable: Participant Happiness Rating

Source	Type III Sum of Squares	df	Mean Square	F	Sig.
Corrected Model	50.538[a]	3	16.846	24.179	.000
Intercept	2111.513	1	2111.513	3030.688	.000
DrugThoughts	2.113	1	2.113	3.032	.086
ConfederateHappyAngry	25.313	1	25.313	36.331	.000
DrugThoughts * ConfederateHappyAngry	23.113	1	23.113	33.174	.000
Error	52.950	76	.697		
Total	2215.000	80			
Corrected Total	103.488	79			

a. R Squared = .488 (Adjusted R Squared = .468)

2. Choose the correct interpretation of the tests of between-subjects effects.

    A. There was one significant main effect, one nonsignificant main effect, and one significant interaction.

    B. There were two significant main effects and one significant interaction.

    C. There were no significant main effects and one significant interaction.

    D. There was one significant main effect, one nonsignificant main effect, and one nonsignificant interaction.

    E. There were two significant main effects and one nonsignificant interaction.

3. Which of the following is the accurate APA format for writing up the main effect result for ConfederateHappyAngry.

    A. We ran a univariate ANOVA with drug (placebo vs. real) and confederate emotion (happy vs. angry) as our two independent variables and participant happiness rating as our dependent variable. There was a significant main effect for confederate emotion, $F(1, 76) = 36.33$, $p < .05$. Participants rated themselves as more happy when they saw a happy confederate ($M = 4.58$, $SD = 0.87$) than when they saw an angry confederate ($M = 5.70$, $SD = 1.11$).

    B. We ran a univariate ANOVA with drug (placebo vs. real) and confederate emotion (happy vs. angry) as our two independent variables and participant happiness rating as our dependent variable. There was no significant main effect for confederate emotion, $F(1, 76) = 3.03$, $p > .05$. Participants did not rate themselves differently when they saw a happy confederate ($M = 5.70$, $SD = 1.11$) compared to an angry confederate ($M = 4.58$, $SD = 0.87$).

    C. We ran a univariate ANOVA with drug (placebo vs. real) and confederate emotion (happy vs. angry) as our two independent variables and participant happiness rating as our dependent variable. There was a significant main effect for confederate emotion, $F(2, 76) = 36.33$, $p < .05$. Participants rated themselves as more happy when they saw a happy confederate ($M = 5.70$, $SD = 1.11$) than when they saw an angry confederate ($M = 4.58$, $SD = 0.87$).

    D. We ran a univariate ANOVA with drug (placebo vs. real) and confederate emotion (happy vs. angry) as our two independent variables and participant happiness rating as our dependent variable. There was a significant main effect for confederate emotion, $F(1, 76) = 36.33$, $p < .001$. Participants rated themselves as more happy when they saw a happy confederate ($M = 5.70$, $SD = 1.11$) than when they saw an angry confederate ($M = 4.58$, $SD = 0.87$).

    E. We ran a univariate ANOVA with drug (placebo vs. real) and confederate emotion (happy vs. angry) as our two independent variables and participant

(Continued)

(Continued)

happiness rating as our dependent variable. There was a significant main effect for confederate emotion, $F(1, 76) = 33.17$, $p < .001$. Participants rated themselves as more happy when they saw a happy confederate ($M = 5.70$, $SD = 1.11$) than when they saw an angry confederate ($M = 4.58$, $SD = 0.87$).

4. Which of the following is the correct write-up for the interaction and (if significant) follow-up simple effects tests?

   A. The interaction was not significant, $F(1, 76) = 33.17$, $p > .05$. Since this is not significant, we would not need to run simple effects follow-up tests.

   B. The interaction was not significant, $F(1, 80) = 3.03$, $p > .05$. Since this is not significant, we would not need to run simple effects follow-up tests.

   C. The interaction was significant, $F(1, 80) = 33.17$, $p < .001$. Since this is significant, we would need to run four simple effects tests. (1) We would look at happy confederates only (seeing if placebo vs. real drug differs). (2) We would look at angry confederates only (seeing if placebo vs. real drug differs). (3) We would look at the placebo drug only (seeing if angry vs. happy confederates differ). (4) Finally, we would look at real drug only (seeing if angry vs. happy confederates differ).

   D. The interaction was significant, $F(1, 76) = 33.17$, $p < .001$. Since this is significant, we would need to run two simple effects tests. (1) We would look at happy confederates only (seeing if placebo vs. real drug differs). (2) We would look at angry confederates only (seeing if placebo vs. real drug differs).

   E. The interaction was significant, $F(1, 76) = 33.17$, $p < .001$. Since this is significant, we would need to run four simple effects tests. (1) We would look at happy confederates only (seeing if placebo vs. real drug differs). (2) We would look at angry confederates only (seeing if placebo vs. real drug differs). (3) We would look at the placebo drug only (seeing if angry vs. happy confederates differ). (4) Finally, we would look at real drug only (seeing if angry vs. happy confederates differ).

5. On the next page is a set of two simple effects tests using the split file function. After looking at the charts, I interpret it this way:

   Following the significant original interaction, $F(1, 76) = 33.17$, $p < .001$, follow-up simple effects tests showed significance for the placebo condition, $F(1, 38) = 41.80$, $p < .001$, with participants rating their own happiness higher in the happy confederate condition ($M = 6.40$, $SD = 1.14$) than the angry confederate condition ($M = 4.20$, $SD = 1.01$). However, the simple effects test was not significant for the real drug condition, $F(1, 38) = .11$, $p = .75$. Thus participants who thought the drug was real did not alter their emotion ratings regardless of whether they saw a happy confederate ($M = 5.00$, $SD = 0.46$) or an angry confederate ($M = 4.95$, $SD = 0.51$).

Is this a correct interpretation of those simple effects tests? Why or why not?

A. Yes, it is a correct interpretation in its entirety. (There was a significant difference between happy and angry in the placebo condition but no significant difference between happy and angry in the real drug condition.)

B. It is partially correct, as both simple effects were actually significant. (There was a significant difference between happy and angry in the placebo condition, and there was a significant difference between happy and angry in the real drug condition.)

C. It is partially incorrect, since neither simple effect was significant. (There was no significant difference between happy and angry in the placebo condition and no significant difference between happy and angry in the real drug condition.)

D. The interpretation is backward. (There was no significant difference between happy and angry in the placebo condition, but there was a significant difference between happy and angry in the real drug condition.)

E. There is not enough information in the tables to determine whether this interpretation is correct.

⇨ Univariate Analysis of Variance

[DataSet0]

Between-Subjects Factors

Drug (Placebo or Effective)			Value Label	N
Thinks Drug is a Placebo	Confederate (Happy or Angry)	1.00	Happy	20
		2.00	Angry	20
Thinks Drug is Real	Confederate (Happy or Angry)	1.00	Happy	20
		2.00	Angry	20

Descriptive Statistics

Dependent Variable: Participant Happiness Rating

Drug (Placebo or Effective)	Confederate (Happy or Angry)	Mean	Std. Deviation	N
Thinks Drug is a Placebo	Happy	6.4000	1.14248	20
	Angry	4.2000	1.00525	20
	Total	5.3000	1.53923	40
Thinks Drug is Real	Happy	5.0000	.45883	20
	Angry	4.9500	.51042	20
	Total	4.9750	.47972	40

Tests of Between-Subjects Effects

Dependent Variable: Participant Happiness Rating

Drug (Placebo or Effective)	Source	Type III Sum of Squares	df	Mean Square	F	Sig.
Thinks Drug is a Placebo	Corrected Model	48.400[a]	1	48.400	41.800	.000
	Intercept	1123.600	1	1123.600	970.382	.000
	ConfederateHappyAngry	48.400	1	48.400	41.800	.000
	Error	44.000	38	1.158		
	Total	1216.000	40			
	Corrected Total	92.400	39			
Thinks Drug is Real	Corrected Model	.025[b]	1	.025	.106	.746
	Intercept	990.025	1	990.025	4203.458	.000
	ConfederateHappyAngry	.025	1	.025	.106	.746
	Error	8.950	38	.236		
	Total	999.000	40			
	Corrected Total	8.975	39			

a. R Squared = .524 (Adjusted R Squared = .511)

b. R Squared = .003 (Adjusted R Squared = -.023)

ANSWER KEY

CHAPTER 1

1. C. Participants ranged in age from 12 to 29 ($M = 20.99$, $SD = 2.82$).

2. B. There were 71 men (49%) and 73 women (51%).

3. D. In this sample, 22 participants were Caucasian (15%), 111 were Hispanic (77%), 3 were African American (2%), 2 were Asian (1%), and 6 did not provide their ethnicity (4%).

4. A. Gender is a nominal variable.

5. A. Age, since it is measured on an interval scale

CHAPTER 2

1. D. Which problem-solving task they received (easy BAT anagram versus impossible-to-solve ORANGE anagram)

2. B. Whether they can rearrange the word CINERAMA

3. C. Only six participants solved the CINERAMA anagram in the hard condition. You can contrast this with 26 participants who solved it in the easy condition.

4. B. For a goodness of fit test we look at only one variable, while we look at more than one variable for a test of independence.

5. D. A chi square test of independence was calculated comparing whether participants solved or did not solve an anagram (CINERAMA). A significant relationship emerged, $\chi^2(1) = 27.70$ $p < .001$. Most participants in the easy anagram condition solved the CINERAMA anagram (86.7%), while very few participants in the hard anagram condition solved the CINERAMA anagram (19.4%). Phi showed a large effect.

CHAPTER 3

1. D. Which problem-solving task they received (hard versus easy anagram)

2. A. Level of frustration

3. E. The easy condition has a mean of 8.37 and standard deviation of 1.30, while the hard condition has a mean of 1.39 and a standard deviation of 0.50.

4. B. Yes, the t-test is significant, $t(59) = 27.89, p < .001$.

5. A. We ran an independent samples t-test with anagram condition as our independent variable and frustration as our dependent variable. The t-test was significant, $t(59) = 27.89, p < .001$. Participants were more frustrated in the hard anagram condition ($M = 1.39, SD = 0.50$) than the easy anagram condition ($M = 8.37, SD = 1.30$).

CHAPTER 4

1. C. The three conditions (60 minutes, 5 minutes, control/no info)

2. A. Participant's willingness to participate in the study

3. D. 5-Minute Condition ($M = 7.93, SD = 0.73$); 60-Minute Condition ($M = 2.07, SD = 0.07$); Control Condition ($M = 5.76, SD = 1.07$)

4. E. It is significant, $F(2, 87) = 364.01, p < .001$.

5. E. We ran a one-way ANOVA with time as our independent variable and willingness as our dependent variable. The one-way ANOVA was significant, $F(2, 87) = 364.01, p < .001$. Tukey post hoc tests revealed that participants were more willing to do the study in the 5-Minute Condition ($M = 7.93, SD = 0.73$) than either the 60-Minute Condition ($M = 2.07, SD = 0.07$) or Control Condition ($M = 5.76, SD = 1.07$). In addition, those in the Control Condition were more willing to participate than those in the 60-Minute Condition.

CHAPTER 5

1. D. There are two independent variables. First, there is a drug manipulation (the participant either thinks the drug is real or thinks it is placebo).

Second, the behavior of the confederate varies (the confederate is either happy or angry). There is one dependent variable: personal rating of happiness.

2. A. There was one significant main effect, one nonsignificant main effect, and one significant interaction.

3. D. We ran a univariate ANOVA with drug (placebo vs. real) and confederate emotion (happy vs. angry) as our two independent variables and participant happiness rating as our dependent variable. There was a significant main effect for confederate emotion, $F(1, 76) = 36.33$, $p < .001$. Participants rated themselves as more happy when they saw a happy confederate ($M = 5.70$, $SD = 1.11$) than when they saw an angry confederate ($M = 4.58$, $SD = 0.87$).

4. E. The interaction was significant, $F(1, 76) = 33.17$, $p < .001$. Since this is significant, we would need to run four simple effects tests. (1) We would look at happy confederates only (seeing if placebo vs. real drug differs). (2) We would look at angry confederates only (seeing if placebo vs. real drug differs). (3) We would look at the placebo drug only (seeing if angry vs. happy confederates differ). (4) Finally, we would look at real drug only (seeing if angry vs. happy confederates differ).

5. A. Yes, it is a correct interpretation in its entirety. (There was a significant difference between happy and angry in the placebo condition but no significant difference between happy and angry in the real drug condition.)